What people ar

Lasting Impact

"I must say that this book by far is Chris's best work to date! This is a must-read for leaders of a family, a business, church or anyone in between, desiring to have an impact with people. I will use this as a resource for many years to come!"

—Greg Provenzano,
President and Co-Founder of ACN Inc.

"My friend Chris Widener has always been a man of impact and personal growth. A wonderful storyteller with a passion for coaching, Chris shares powerful insights from his own life and the lives of others on how to improve your life and live it with authentic impact. His latest gem is a must-read."

—Waldo Waldman,
Author of the New York Times and
Wall Street Journal Best Seller *Never Fly Solo*

"Anytime I have an opportunity to learn from Chris, I jump on it because I always get so many insights and 'aha' moments. Reading this book was no different. Chris's writing style is so captivating I had a hard time putting it down and absolutely loved it. This is one that's worth reading multiple times."

—Matt Morris,
Bestselling Author of *The Unemployed Millionaire*

"*Lasting Impact* is a powerful book. I have invested the last ten years focusing on legacy and I believe strongly that if you want to leave a legacy by design and not by chance, then you need to devour *Lasting Impact*."

—Tom Ziglar,
CEO of Zig Ziglar, Author and Speaker

"Chris has a lifetime of business and personal experience, and he shares stories that will make you think and move you to action! This book spoke to me in ways that most don't. It's one of the greatest lessons in personal development that I have ever read!"

—Jordan Adler,
**Author of the Amazon Best Seller *Beach Money*,
Network Marketing Millionaire and Dream Broker**

"If you've ever asked yourself, 'What will be my legacy?', this is the book for you. *Lasting Impact* takes you far beyond traditional business and self-help books because the principles are timeless. And more importantly, the results will be timeless."

—Stephen Shapiro, Author
of *Invisible Solutions*

"For over 15 years, Chris Widener has been a major influence in my business and my life. The principles explained in this book are carefully crafted to impact anyone seeking a life of significance."

—Ryan D. Chamberlin,
Author and Communicator

"Warning! Do not attempt to read this book. No, your mission is to *learn* from the book. This is the book you need to devour page by page to fully understand each lesson shared. You'll find yourself making notes and highlighting each page. To take a quote from Chris, 'You were made to make an impact.' That's what you will do as a result of spending time with *Lasting Impact*."

—**Mark Hunter,**
"The Sales Hunter" and Author of *A Mind for Sales*

"'What's the point of it all?' I think this is a question that most people ask themselves at some point in their lives. In *Lasting Impact*, Chris Widener gives you ways to find the point and purpose in your life and take action. My favorite books inspire me, challenge me, and make me think. Chris does a great job with all three."

—**Joe Calloway,**
Author of *The Leadership Mindset*

"There are people who make no impact, those that impact, and those that create *lasting* impact. Chris Widener is in the last group. He's built a large circle of influence, and in this book, he breaks down how he did it—and how you can make your own lasting impact!"

—**Randy Gage,**
Author of New York Times Best Sellers
Risky Is the New Safe **and** *Mad Genius*

"Apparently being immortal isn't an option. Fortunately, we can instead opt-in for a lasting legacy. If that sounds good to you, then you'll enjoy Chris Widener's fast-moving book on that exact subject. Each chapter has an unexpected story from Chris's life or the experiences of his friends and mentors. Give it a read!"

—Brian Walter, CSP, CPAE,
Infotainer, Speaker and Communications Consultant
at Extreme Meetings Inc.

"My life has always been about making an impact, and it has been quite the journey of ups and downs. Thankfully, I learned lessons along the way that have enabled me to make a worldwide impact. Chris's book, *Lasting Impact*, will help you cut your learning curve down so you can make an impact on the people you touch during your time here and understand how to navigate the obstacles that may get in your way. Filled with fascinating real-life examples, you won't be able to put this powerful book down!"

—Eric Worre,
Founder of Network Marketing Pro

"You don't learn the best lessons from those who have simply been successful, but from those who have overcome great challenges to be successful. Chris Widener's story will inspire and encourage you, and his ideas will enable you to go beyond success to make a lasting impact."

—Mark Sanborn,
Bestselling Author of *The Fred Factor* and
You Don't Need a Title to Be a Leader

"If you are ready for exponential impact, read, absorb, and use the wisdom in this book now!"

—Mark Victor Hansen,
Co-creator of the *Chicken Soup for the Soul* series,
the *One Minute Millionaire* series, and the *Ask* series

"It is the desire of every true leader to inspire others and leave a lasting positive impact in the world as your legacy. Chris Widener shares with you some amazing principles to do just that! His chapter on impacting the impactors is simply brilliant and on point! This is a MUST-READ!"

—Erik Swanson,
Keynote Speaker, Bestselling Author and
CEO of Habitude Warrior Int.

"I have found that most people go through life looking for secrets to living a life of impact and purpose. Chris Widener has written a book that gives you powerful insights into achieving a life that makes an impact! *Lasting Impact* by my friend Chris Widener is a book that will help you make that big impact on the world! Read it and share it…you will be glad you did!"

—Dr. Willie Jolley, Hall of Fame Speaker,
National TV and Radio Personality and
Bestselling Author of *A Setback Is a Setup For a Comeback*
and *An Attitude of Excellence*

"Chris Widener has lived and breathed the process of success for decades now, and has mastered the process of leaving an optimistic impact on the world. Do yourself a favor and stand on the shoulders of a success giant and follow his principles to make a lasting impact in the world!"

—Tripp Hammett, President
of Hammett Gravel

LASTING
IMPACT

How to Create a Life and Business That Lives Beyond You

Chris Widener

Made for Success
PUBLISHING

Made for Success Publishing
P.O. Box 1775 Issaquah, WA 98027
www.MadeForSuccessPublishing.com

Distributed by Made for Success Publishing

First Printing
Library of Congress Cataloging-in-Publication data
Widener, Chris
Lasting Impact: How to Create a Life and Business
That Lives Beyond You

p. cm.

LCCN: 2020940792
ISBN: 978-1-64146-476-5 (Paperback)
ISBN: 978-1-64146-536-6 (ebook)
ISBN: 978-1-64146-519-9 (Audiobook)

Printed in the United States of America

For further information contact Made for Success Publishing
+14255266480 or email service@madeforsuccess.net

Dedicated to my beautiful wife, Denise.
I am thankful every day for the lasting
impact you have had on my life.

Table of Contents

Foreword

by Larry Winget

Several years ago, my wife and I had a New Year's Eve party at our house. A friend of ours wore a beautiful dress that was covered in some kind of gold, glitter-like stuff. Every place she sat ended up with glitter on it. Even the rugs had glitter on them. My friend left a shiny residue wherever she went. The sofa and chairs have been cleaned and vacuumed several times since then, and the area rugs have been shampooed a few times as well. I have even moved houses three times since the party. Know what? The glitter residue lives on! Her appearance at my party had an impact, and the residue from her presence had a lasting impact. I will not forget her being at my party. The truth is, I can't forget because of all that glitter. Her presence left something behind that will, evidently, last forever. How about you, your life, your presence? Will it last?

You live, you die. Your time on earth ends. There is no way to avoid it, regardless of how hard you try. It happens to every person. It is completely unavoidable.

This little fact, as painful as it might be, must be accepted at some point. And in accepting this fact, it seems to me that the concern for every person comes down to a handful of questions:

"Did I make a difference?"

"Will I be remembered?"

"What will I be remembered for?"

We all search for a certain level of comfort that comes from knowing that what we did in our short time here will last past our funeral. To put it simply, we want to make an impact.

We all want our words, our actions, our contribution and our presence to have an impact while we are here, and to last after we are gone. I believe that every person who has ever drawn a breath wants that.

I have written a bunch of bestselling books. I've sold a couple of million copies of those books. Over the past thirty years, I have spoken to audiences all over the world. I appear regularly on television shows that are seen by millions of people. You would think I would be confident that I have a lock on having a lasting impact. Nope. I know firsthand the temporary public infatuation that comes with fame. There is always a new flavor of the day in every area of life and business. I never fool myself in how long fame lasts.

Luckily, I know that fame, number of speeches given, size of audience and number of books sold have very little, if anything, to do with creating a lasting impact. And be clear, I am not being overly modest, nor am I bragging in any way. I am proud of my work, and I know the things I have done have had an impact. But, whether the impact will be *lasting* is questionable.

Because fame is not impact. Impact, especially lasting impact, is more.

Sadly, too many focus on fame, how much money they have, their job and their stuff, and have fooled themselves into thinking those things are what will create a lasting impact. They are wrong. Those things might create an impact, but I seriously doubt that impact will last.

In my case, lasting impact is created by focusing on the moment and not the future. Those who focus on the future end up wasting the present. That's why I think that having an impact after you are gone can only be done by paying attention to what you are doing every day, every moment … right now. It's based on living core values that create a reputation you are known for. A reputation based on your interaction with individuals that influences their behavior through their thoughts and actions that then carries on through their interaction with other individuals—and on and on and on. That's how an impact lasts.

So, how do you do it? How do you live your life so you have the answers to the questions I just mentioned? How do you give meaning and purpose to your life so it will have a lasting impact? Luckily, my friend Chris has written this book to show you how. Pay attention to his words. Think about the stories he tells about his life and the examples he uses of others. Think about how you can use them to alter your thoughts, words and actions so they will have an impact that lasts. Read the book. Heed the book. Create a life that matters now and always will. Create a life that leaves a gold glitter residue that can't be forgotten.

Introduction

I've had a crazy life. As I write this, I'm 53 years old and, believe me; it's been quite a ride. Let me tell you about it.

I was born in 1966 into an affluent home in Seattle, Washington. My father was a partner at NBBJ, which, at the time, was a large, regional architecture firm, but now has become one of the biggest and most influential architecture firms in the world. In fact, they designed the brand-new Google headquarters. My dad was the CFO of the firm.

In 1969, my dad made $90,000. Many people today would love to make $90,000, but in 1969, that was what a friend of mine calls, "gangster money."

In 1970, my dad died of cancer. They discovered it in May, and he died in November. Of course, that was devastating, but to add to the devastation, my dad only had $30,000 worth of life insurance. So, he left my mother and his children in quite a conundrum. The home that we lived in was the biggest and most beautiful home in the Sand Point Country Club. It overlooked the golf course, Lake Washington, and in the distance, the Cascade mountain range. That home sold in 2013 for 1.88 million dollars. Unfortunately, at the time, my mother couldn't afford the $400 mortgage repayments, so we moved to a small condominium on the other side of town.

Thus, began my downward spiral. I did not handle the adversity well. I began to act out in school and cause problems. My brothers and sisters were considerably older than me, and they were out of the home shortly after my dad died. Because of the distance between the ages of my closest sibling and me, I guess you could say I was an "oops" baby.

I'll give you the brief overview of the head-spinning years that were my childhood. I moved dozens of times, went to 11 different schools, and was shipped off to live with relatives twice, once in the fourth grade and again in the ninth grade.

One day, in the fourth grade, my mother and I were in the car and began heading east out of Seattle on I-90. I asked her where we were going, and she told me that we were going to visit my Uncle Paul and Aunt Rochelle. I was happy with that because I liked my Uncle Paul and Aunt Rochelle. But, when I asked my mother how long we were staying, her answer was strange. She told me that she was going to be staying two hours.

Now, in the fourth grade, you haven't perfected your deductive reasoning skills yet, but I knew something wasn't right. I asked how long I was staying, and I was told that I was going to be staying with my Aunt Rochelle and my Uncle Paul for two years.

My Uncle Paul was a log truck driver and was nearly a caricature of what you would think a wild truck driver would look like. He had a big, bushy beard, weighed about 250 pounds, and wore big red suspenders to keep his jeans up. He donned these big boots that you would wear in the woods. Funny enough, my Aunt Rochelle was also a log truck driver. Her nickname was Sarge, and she had 50 pounds on my Uncle Paul.

The idea was they were going to whip me into shape—emphasis on the whip. Well, I proved to be too much to handle, even for my Aunt Rochelle and my Uncle Paul. They sent me home to my mother after the fifth grade.

I began to use drugs and alcohol in the sixth grade and made most of my money betting the horses at Longacre's Racetrack and scalping professional sporting event tickets outside of the arenas. In the ninth grade, I was shipped off to live with my sister and her husband, a Seattle police officer. In the tenth grade, I received 47 written referrals to the principal's office. My mentor, Zig Ziglar, used to say that he "graduated in the half of the class that made the top half possible." Well, I graduated in the 10% of the class that made the other 90% possible. I barely got out of high school and into college.

Can you see that I was going nowhere fast?

Shortly before my senior year of high school, I met a youth worker who opened my eyes to a whole new world. First of all, he talked to me about God, which gave me a better understanding of the fact that there was a purpose for my life. That was when I began to think about the idea that I may have been put here to accomplish something. It was mind-blowing. And it completely revolutionized my life.

I graduated from college and began to work as a youth worker in a small, wealthy Northern New Jersey town called Mendham. It was there that I met some of the most successful men and women in America. I met them because their kids were in my youth group. Many of these people had a profound impact on my life by teaching me how to have a vision and a purpose and pursue it relentlessly with excellence. My three years in Mendham, New Jersey, were three years that significantly shaped my life because of the mentoring I received from them—people who were making a lasting impact on the world.

I ended up spending 11 years as a minister in churches in the Seattle area, and then began writing and speaking full-time in 2002. It was at that time that I met and began working with John Maxwell.

My life has had lots of ups and downs. I've made a lot of money, and I've lost a lot of money. I bought my dream home in the Cascade Mountains outside of Seattle, where my front gate was 500 feet long and made out of brick pillars and wrought iron fencing. It was on 10 acres with a half a mile of riverfront, a swimming pool, and a pool house. It even had an 1,800-bottle wine cellar.

Unfortunately, four years after I bought it, it started collapsing into the river. It was about then that my marriage started collapsing as well. I was married for 27 years before we divorced, and the pain was devastating. However, I have four beautiful children and four wonderful grandchildren because of it. I also have a great daughter-in-law and two terrific stepsons.

Recently, I married my incredible wife, Denise, who really helped me regain my life and purpose. Denise has two beautiful daughters who have become my stepdaughters, and I love them as my own. Denise and I have recently released a book together called *Better the Second Time: How to Have an Amazing Second Marriage*.

Throughout this life, I have had many amazing accomplishments. I've written a New York Times and Wall Street Journal best-selling book. I've spoken thousands of times all over the world in fantastic places like China, Singapore, Russia, Egypt, Australia, Spain, Germany, and all over the United States. I have met incredible people who have equally incredible accomplishments. I had my own television show. I was personally mentored by two of the greatest legends in the speaking business, Jim Rohn, who I spent the last seven years of his life with, and Zig Ziglar, with whom I co-hosted the television show, *True Performance*. I even ran for the United States Senate in 2010 in the state of Washington!

Yes, it's been quite a life.

But do you know what has driven much of my adult life? The desire to make an impact. It really is the most important thing to me. Far more important than money. As a speaker, we get paid really well to come and give speeches, but that's not why I do it. At every speech, I try to make an impact. The bigger the crowd, the better. I've had the great privilege to speak to crowds of 10,000, 15,000, 20,000, and even 25,000 people. It's incredible to stand in front of that many people and speak words of life and success into their lives and challenge them to make their own impact.

Decades ago, I wrote my own personal mission statement, which says:

I will use my writing and speaking skills to help other people turn their potential and performance, succeed in every area of their lives, and achieve their dreams.

That will be my impact. And it has driven everything that I have done for the last 30 years. If it doesn't involve me writing or speaking, I probably won't do it. If it doesn't lead to the outcome of helping other people with their own lives, I probably will not be involved. Everything about my life is about making an impact. I guess you could say that I want people to feel it when I'm gone!

I hope you enjoy this book and that it makes an impact on you and causes you to think about your impact on others. I have some great stories in here, and I highlight some very special people—both well-known and not so well-known—who are making a tremendous impact.

Here's to your impact!

Chapter One

The Quest for Impact

I believe that everybody wants to make an impact with their life. Yes, there will be some who will lose vision for what their life could become, but most people are focused on what they can accomplish in their time here on earth.

You could say that eternity is in our hearts. It is within men and women to want to make their lives matter; the irony being that everyone knows that their time will eventually be up. It's your ambition and what you're best at doing set against the futility of knowing that no matter what you do, you will eventually stop doing it.

We all want to know that we matter. We want to know that our life makes a difference. We want to know that if we weren't here, the world would be a little bit worse off. We want to know that our work affects other people.

At the 1999 Super Bowl, online job search company Monster ran a tongue-in-cheek, satirical commercial about what kids wanted to be when they grow up. It showed one child after another delivering these lines. Here is the transcript of that commercial:

When I Grow Up
When I grow up, I want to file all day.
I want to climb my way up to middle management.
Be replaced on a whim.
I want to have a brown nose.
I want to be a "yes" man.
A "yes" woman.
Yes, Sir. Coming, sir.
I'll do anything for a raise, sir.
When I grow up, I want to be underappreciated.
Be paid less for doing the same job.

Yeah, right! Who wants that? Nobody. We want mission, possibility, and opportunity. We want to do something that matters!

This isn't about fame. This is about purpose. Yes, many people in our day and age confuse the two. There's a whole generation of social media influencers who believe that fame is impact. It can be, but it isn't always. I suppose you can make the argument that there is impact no matter what, whether it be good, bad, or indifferent.

Unfortunately, I believe that too many people mistake fame for impact and so they become prolific on social media, thinking that is the way to make a difference in the lives of others. It certainly can be, and my hundreds of thousands of social media followers do enjoy my posts, I'm sure, but reach doesn't equal influence and impact.

So, what is this longing within men and women? I believe that it's rooted in the fact that we know that we're all going to die someday. It becomes part race, part attempt to prove our own value.

I know that this sense of impending death has affected me my entire life. I became aware of the brevity of life at a very early age. As mentioned before, my dad, who was 41 at the time, passed away in 1970, when I was just 4 years old. That made me very aware of how someone can be there one day, gone forever the next. This made a profound impact on the way I lived my own life and gave me insight into the psychology of people and their desire to live in such a way as to leave a legacy.

Jim Rohn said in his book *Twelve Pillars* that we cannot determine how long we live, but we can determine how *well* we live. How long you live is a matter for higher powers. How well you live is completely and totally up to you. We can't determine whether we're going to get sick today or hit by a bus tomorrow, but we can determine that whatever we do today, we will do with integrity and excellence to leave the world a better place than we found it this morning.

I have a brother who is 13 years older than me. He had a funny interaction with my mother on his 41st birthday. She called him up to wish him a happy birthday and asked him how he was doing. He said that he was doing really well, but then he confessed that for the past year, he had been a little fearful that he might die. My mother asked him why, and he said that when he turned 40, he was afraid that he would die because Dad was 40 when he died. My mother, who couldn't leave well enough alone, replied, "Oh, your dad wasn't 40 when he died. He was 41!" Then my brother spent *another* year worried that his life would be cut short before he could do all that he wanted to do.

We want to know that our actions help others. We want to know that our thoughts contribute to solutions. We want to know that our words build others up rather than tear them down. We want to know that what we do on a daily basis is something that contributes in a greater way to the overall good of society.

So, how do we do it? How do we live in such a way that our lives make a difference beyond us? How do we build a business that continues on after we pass away, helping people long after we are gone? What exactly can we do to ensure that, by the time we are on our deathbed, we are filled with nothing but the satisfaction of knowing that we have done well, both for ourselves and for others?

I believe that it comes from a combination of our character, the way we show up, the values we hold, actions we take, the skills we contribute, and, yes, things we have no control over. Some might call it serendipity. Christians may call it God's sovereignty. Malcolm Gladwell may suggest that it is a random Tipping Point, and no one knows why it happened. We do everything that we can do, and the rest is up to something else.

Still, the first part of the equation is so powerful. Everything we can do is certainly within our power.

Character includes traits like integrity, commitment to excellence, a servant-minded heart, optimism, perseverance, and ambition. These are the internal things that move us forward. Some people simply have more ambition than others and, therefore, they will do more good *for* others. This isn't a bad or good thing. It just is. Take two people with equal skills and equal character, but give one more ambition, and he or she will move the world in ways that the other won't.

Skills, on the other hand, are things like how well you handle your money, build your business, and communicate. While character is who you are, your skills are what you do. My mentor, Zig Ziglar, had an equation for achieving what it is that you wanted to achieve. It was:

Be. Do. Have.

Most people start with what they want to have, then they ask a question: What do I need to do in order to have that? Zig knows there are more than just your actions involved. Your character matters. Who you *are* drives what you *do*. Asking what to do in order to have what we want to have leaves out the foundational aspect of character.

First, you must *have* to *be*. Most people do not give much thought to who they are. The inner life is something that all too many people avoid. As it was put so powerfully by the great philosopher Socrates, "The unexamined life is not worth living."

Don't get me wrong; the over-examined life isn't worth living either. You can spend too much time thinking. But that doesn't seem to be the problem for the majority of modern Americans. Most of us are a mile wide and an inch deep. People who have impact plunge to the depths.

Are you taking time for yourself? Are you doing the deep inner work that will make you a person of impact? We are definitely an Instagram society. Flashy, colorful, covered with masks that show others what we want them to see. All done in the blink of an eye in order to create a perception that, most times, isn't really accurate at all. It's important for the person of impact to take time for him or herself. Get alone. Think. Reflect.

One of the great disciplines I've seen is in a friend of mine, the New York Times and Wall Street Journal bestselling author and leadership guru, Mark Sanborn. Mark spends at least 15 minutes a day with nothing but himself, a legal pad, and a pen. Sometimes it lasts much longer than 15 minutes, but Mark has disciplined himself for decades to spend at least 15 minutes a day reflecting and thinking.

Ziglar did the same thing. For decades, he spent three hours a day reading. He says that reading time is what filled him up so he could pour out to so many others during his speeches. It's no wonder then that Zig rose to become the highest-paid public speaker before he passed away at $100,000 a speech.

What are you reading? It's been said that we become like the books we read and the people we hang around with. So, let me ask you again: What are you reading? Does your reading list consist of *People* magazine or *Sports Illustrated* with the occasional beach detective novel thrown in? People of impact are not concerned with the frivolities of life. They're concerned with substance. This doesn't mean that you have to be a nuclear scientist or astrophysicist, but it *does* mean that you have to push yourself to learn about the meaning and purpose of life.

If you are going to make an impact, you're going to have to start out with some idea of what that impact is. Some people decide that they're going to go into politics. Others decide that they're going to move halfway around the world and work with malnourished children. Others decide to become emergency room nurses and others, police officers. It doesn't matter how you make your impact in this world, or through what profession. Rather, the likelihood of you making a significant impact has a direct correlation to your purposefulness in picking that outlet for your impact.

It takes all of us to make change happen. We can't all do the same thing and make an impact in the same way. In many ways, our impact works together. The man who owns the gas station makes an impact by allowing people to travel and get to where they need to go. He serves the police officer putting gas in his car so he can take his daughter to daycare so he can go off and protect us. The caretaker who takes care of the police officer's child makes a difference and impact in that child's life and society by supporting the impact mission of the police officer. And, of course, the police officer makes an impact by protecting us once he has his child safe and sound with the babysitter. All three of them are loosely connected in the morning before the police officer's shift, and all are playing their specific part in making an impact.

My friend Waldo Waldman, one of the most successful speakers and authors in America today, tells a story of when he was a fighter pilot in the United States Air Force. For some reason, after one of these flights, he got angry at one of the young linemen who worked on his airplane, preparing it for Waldo to fly. He was less than gracious with that young man. Shortly thereafter, Waldo's commander called him in and let him know in no uncertain terms that he should never treat that young lineman that way ever again. He reiterated to Waldo that they are all part of the same team. Waldo confesses— and this is a confession that many of us could make—that he thought that his place of impact was more important than someone else's. Nothing could be further from the truth. We all tie in together.

One person chooses to be the gas station owner, another chooses to be a childcare worker, another chooses to be a police officer, another chooses to be a fighter pilot, and another chooses to be a lineman, working on airplanes. Doesn't matter what you do. But it does matter that you know exactly what you *want* to do.

Stephen Covey, in his book *The Seven Habits of Highly Effective People,* said that we should begin with the end in mind. Before you ever begin, do you know where you're going? Of course, things don't always end up working out the way we want them to, and I cover that in detail in one chapter of this book, but for the most part, we can choose where we want to go and then begin our journey there.

Do you know what your purpose is? Do you know your life's mission for making an impact? Do you know what it will take to get there? Are you willing to do what it would take to get there?

Once you decide what you want to do to make your impact, you have to have a strategy for getting there. Whether it is going to university and getting the education it takes to do your dream job or starting a business or nonprofit, you have to lay out the strategy for executing your impact plan.

I would suggest establishing long-range goals, mid-range goals, and short-term goals. Once you've established where you want to go in the long, mid- and short range, you can establish the strategy for getting there. I like to think of this like going on a road trip and charting it out on a map. I choose the ultimate destination first and then map out the cities and towns I will need to stop in on the way to get to my ultimate destination.

This makes the process a lot simpler because if I know I'm going to the ultimate destination, I know my shorter-term tasks are on my way to get to the first, then the second, and so on. That's how I actually execute my strategy. So, if you were talking about a non-profit you want to raise a million dollars a year for, you would establish by what year you want to raise $1,000,000. Then you can establish your one-year goal, your three-year goal, and so on.

Once your goals are established, you have to have a strategy. To take our non-profit fundraising goal example, your strategy could be to get a thousand people to give $1,000 a year. That would be $1,000,000. Or it could be to get 2,000 people to give $500 a year. Most likely, it will be some mixture of the levels of giving that will help you attain your goal. Then you might have different strategies for how you're going to reach those people. You might do in-person events, email blasts, or online advertising. The idea is that you have to have a plan and a strategy.

First, begin with the end in mind; second, establish your goals and a strategy for meeting them, and third, execute.

There was an article written a long time ago about the number one downfall of CEOs in America. The authors mentioned that prior to writing the article, they assumed that the biggest downfall for CEOs would be a lack of vision. However, what they found out was that it was a lack of *execution*. Vision is the easy part. Establishing where you want to go and setting a dream for it is simple. But the day-to-day execution on the front lines is where most people fail. Any sort of impact is going to require long-term, day-to-day grinding it out. The mundane will certainly be more frequent than the spectacular. The goal is that the mundane tasks add up to the accomplishment of the impact you want to have on the world.

I'm writing this book because I want you to think big about your life and the impact you will leave on the people you come in contact with. I'm writing this book because I believe in the power of impact. So many people have impacted my life profoundly, and I, in turn, have impacted many through my books and speeches.

Whether it is those closest to me, or one of the tens of thousands of people who might sit in an audience, I want to know that my life, philosophies, words, and actions challenge others to become better and to make a difference. That is how I leave my impact—challenging and encouraging *you* to make your impact. Throughout the rest of this book, we're going to take a look at those things we must master in order to make our impact.

Questions for Reflection:

How would you describe your quest for impact?

Does the knowledge of your eventual death cause you to think more about your impact while you're here? How so?

What are your thoughts about the *Be, Do, Have* equation? Do you agree? Why or why not?

Do you know what your life purpose is? What is it?

Have you established your goals? What are your short-, mid-, and long-range goals?

Chapter Two

It's Just as Easy to Think Big as It Is to Think Small

"There is no passion to be found playing small, in settling for a life that is less than the one you are capable of living."

— Nelson Mandela

If there is one thing that I am known for saying, it would be, "It's just as easy to think big as it is to think small." People ask me on podcast interviews and radio interviews all the time if I have one last piece of advice I'd like to leave with people, and it is always the same. It's just as easy to think big as it is to think small.

Big thinkers change the world. Big thinkers make progress. Big thinkers move people to greater achievement. We need big thinkers. Big thinkers are the ones that make a big impact. Small thinkers make small impacts.

Don't get me wrong; a small impact is still great. One of the key elements for us to understand is that the size of your impact doesn't make you any better as a person. It is simply a testament to the size of the impact you've made. This book isn't for those who want to play small. This is for people who want to play big. They want to make a big difference and a big impact. In order to do that, you have to think big.

If You Can't Join Them, Beat Them...

I met a girl in the 7th grade who would end up becoming a lifelong friend (and who I would later help with her speaking business). Her name is Michelle Akers.

When she was a little girl, Michelle was already a big thinker. What was her big dream? To play on the Pittsburgh Steelers! She really thought it was her destiny. But, there were other plans at work for Michelle's life.

Michelle grew up to become the greatest female soccer player of all time (sorry, Mia). Michelle was a pioneer for female sports in general, but more specifically, soccer. FIFA named 125 players on their 100th anniversary as the greatest soccer players of all time, and there were only two women on that entire list. There were also only two Americans on that list, and both Americans were those two women. One was Mia Hamm, and the other was Michelle Akers. She was also named the FIFA female player of the century.

Michelle is currently fourth on the all-time scoring list, which is a little bit deceptive because she moved from striker to midfielder in 1991, where she spent the balance of her career to protect her from the beatings she was taking from opposing players and concussions. Had she stayed at striker, she would have probably set an unattainable record.

Michelle was on numerous United States Olympic and World Cup teams, including 1999, where they beat China in the finals. That was likely the game that put the US Women's Soccer Team on the map for good.

Michelle was a big dreamer. And when one big dream proved itself unattainable, she set her sights on another: becoming the world's greatest soccer player.

Oh, and while she never fulfilled her dream of playing for the Pittsburgh Steelers, in the early 1990s, the Dallas Cowboys asked her to kick field goals for them—which she declined in order to play soccer!

Flower Pots for Sale

I've always been a big thinker. My first memory of really thinking big was when I was just a teenager. I believe I was about 14 years old. My mother was working at Group Health Hospital in Seattle, Washington, at the campus on Capitol Hill. She worked with a gentleman who was in medical record filing. This meant that all day long, five days a week, his sole job was to take medical files and walk into a room and sort them alphabetically. We're talking tens of thousands of medical files.

Naturally, he was looking for a way out of this job. He had a wealthy uncle, so he reached out to him and borrowed $7,000 to pay a licensing fee to a national company for the Pacific

Northwest region's rights to sell a self-watering flower pot. Now, don't laugh. This was actually a real thing, and it really worked! This co-worker of my mom's knew me because I would often come to her place of work toward the end of the day. One day, he asked me if I would like to make some extra money selling flower pots. I asked him how much he would pay me, and he told me $1 per pot. I was in business!

Now, what would the typical 14-year-old do in this situation? I believe that the typical 14-year-old would grab a bunch of pots and start going door to door, knocking at every house and selling a few flower pots to grandmas with a green thumb.

Not me…

I called a large regional home improvement store based in my hometown of Seattle. I told them that I had a self-watering flower pot and that I would like to show it to one of their buyers. I'm sure they didn't know I was 14, so they accepted my offer, and an appointment was set. My mother took me to buy my first blue blazer for the sales call, and she dropped me off on a street corner in downtown Seattle in front of their building.

Once in front of the buyer, I pulled the two pieces of the flower pot apart and demonstrated it to him. The bottom part was simply a bowl where you put the water. The top part was another bowl, but it had a stem that went down into the bottom bowl to suck up water based on where the lever was moved to on the side of the pot. If you turned it all the way to the left, it barely took in any water. Turn it all the way to the right, and it took in quite a bit of water. You would set this based on what kind of flower was in the pot and how often it needed to be watered.

The buyer was very impressed. If I remember correctly, they had about 120 stores total in the Pacific Northwest region. The buyer told me that he wanted to do a one-year test run of the flower pots. Each box contained 24 flower pots, and he wanted four boxes of flower pots at each of his 20 stores for a year. Now, let's do the math. 24 times 4 times 20 times 12. That's 23,040 flower pots—just for the test run! My very first sales call, as a 14-year-old kid, made me a $23,040 commission! It was incredible. What happened next... well, it's just sad.

I went back to the gentleman who owned the company and told him that I sold some pots. He asked me how many and I told him I secured an order for 23,040 flower pots. Do you know what he did? He panicked. He wasn't used to success. He didn't know what to do, so he called the flower pot company back up and told them that he wanted to give up his license and wanted a refund of the $7,000. I'm not kidding. You can't make this stuff up. He was so afraid of success—which, ironically, was the very thing he was trying to pursue—that he gave up his new business *and* the money.

When you think about it, I had a choice. Was I going to think small and sell one or two pots at a time door to door, or was I going to go to one buyer and sell 23,040 pots? Now, I said that it's just as easy to think big as it is to think small, and that's true, but it was actually even easier to make the sale of 23,000 pots than it would have been to sell a hundred pots door to door.

Another lesson in thinking big came later on in life. In the early 2000s, a good friend of mine and I decided to create audio programs to sell through large box stores like Costco and Sam's Club. We spent an entire summer on the phone licensing audio programs from professional speakers on a wide variety of topics. We then put them in two boxes with fourteen CDs and one DVD. Now, we could have easily sold those on a website. We could have sold them in the back of the room, which we did at speeches. But that would have been thinking small. Instead, we made a sales call to Costco. Not only did they buy, but eventually, Sam's Club bought as well. Borders and Barnes & Noble bought. And, of course, we were also selling on Amazon.

Soon after getting our program up and running, we were selling between 50,000 and 75,000 boxes a month through Costco and Sam's Club. We could have tried to sell them anywhere, but we decided the best place would be to sell them through the biggest venue we could find. It was quite lucrative. Shortly thereafter, I sold that company to my business partner, and he has since taken it on to make an even bigger impact—not only through audio program publishing, but book publishing as well.

Like Father Like Son

It's always rewarding to see your children grow up to make a difference in the world. Giving them direction as children to make an impact and then seeing them do it is something that makes a father proud.

My son, Chris Widener Jr., is becoming quite an impactor himself. He's 29 as I write this and is the CEO of a brand-new tech startup. He raised $500,000 from investors on the idea, built out the technology, and started bringing in customers. He did a million dollars in his first nine months in business and is now in his second round of fundraising to scale it. It is a business that helps churches and nonprofits raise money for their work. His goal is to serve tens of thousands of churches and nonprofits by helping them raise money in a more effective and less expensive way, thus enabling them to put more money toward their mission. I think that, as a young man, is an incredibly big vision!

So, I have given you a number of examples of big thinking, but what are the keys to thinking big? I think there are a few thoughts to consider.

First of all, you've got to think bigger. You probably already have something in mind in regard to what you want to do to make an impact. That's fantastic! Now, just think bigger. Let's say you want to raise one million dollars a year for charity. That's great. Make it two million dollars a year. What if you really stretch yourself and set a long-term goal of five million dollars a year? Setting big goals will stretch you and, in turn, will cause you to become what it takes to achieve that goal.

Second, consider your capacity. Let's say you are a singer. But, let's say you're not a world-class singer. You don't have the capacity to be Mick Jagger, Bono, Celine Dion, or Bruce Springsteen. That's okay. The capacity that those people have is incredible, but not widely distributed! We have to be honest with ourselves when we're setting our big goals. Maybe you won't be playing sold-out stadium events all around the world, but maybe you do have the capacity to be in a popular local band. And trust me, even small local bands make a difference. There's a local band here in the Scottsdale area that plays a lot of different venues around town. They have a whole group of people that go and watch them and enjoy them. That is, even though it's small, an impact. They know their capacity, and they are good with that.

Third, bring together your resources. Resources can be money, of course, but can also be people, organizations, and other businesses. How will you leverage these resources in order to make your impact? Take a good long look at your resource list and make sure that you have what it takes to get you there. The analogy that I like to think about is climbing Mount Everest. In 2002, I put on a conference in Bellevue, Washington, called Extraordinary Leaders. I brought in, among other speakers, Jim Whittaker, the first American to climb Mount Everest.

While I'm not a mountain climber at all, I am fascinated by people who achieve big things. And getting up Mount Everest is a big deal! One particularly interesting detail I picked up on in reading Jim's book was that it took 900 sherpas to get him up that mountain. He got the glory of being the first American up Mount Everest, but there were 900 other people who got him there!

Interestingly enough, getting up Mount Everest today requires far fewer people because of the advances in technology and gear. The point is, if you are just going to go up a hill in your neighborhood, you probably don't have to think about the resources to get you up to the top. But, if you're going to think big and try to get up Mount Everest, you're going to have to assess and line up your required resources. What resources will your big-impact dream require?

Lastly, you must execute. It is those who maintain their discipline and execute every day who succeed in the long run. My mentor Jim Rohn always said that, "Everyone must experience one of two pains, the pain of discipline or the pain of regret." You can either discipline yourself day in and day out and have no regret, or you can choose the regret that will come from not disciplining yourself and executing your plan. You only get one life. The more you delay, the less likely you are to execute your impact plan.

As I close out this chapter about thinking big, I'm obviously encouraging you to lift your eyes up and see the possibilities, but I also want to assure you that whatever size your impact ends up being, that's okay. There are different levels of impact. I call this Impact Scale.

Some people will impact the world for long after their lifetime. These are what I call *legendary impactors*. These are people like Jesus, Columbus, Michelangelo, and Mother Teresa. These are the people everyone knows—their impact is renowned. Years after their death, sometimes even hundreds or thousands of years afterward, people still know who they are and what they did. There are not very many people at all that fall into this category.

The next category is what I call *world impactors*. These are people who are world-famous. They have a considerable impact, but are not going to end up "legends," per se. These are people like presidents of countries, rock stars, or famous athletes.

The next are what I would call *national impactors*. These are people who will impact their country. Others outside their country may never even know their names, but the millions of people in their respective countries will.

Smaller than national impactors are *regional impactors*. These are people who might impact a state or a few states. These would be people who own regional-sized businesses. Or maybe they are a local personality with some regional recognition. This would be somebody like a newscaster who is well known in a region. They likely use their popularity or notoriety to raise money for charities.

Smaller still are *local impactors*. Now, again, don't believe for a second that because you are only a local impactor that you are somehow a second-rate impactor. All impactors are important! A local impactor would be someone like a local high school teacher, little league coach, or a family who has owned the popular store in town for 40 years.

Lastly, are *family impactors*. The family is the smallest social group we have in the world. Our family of origin is incredibly powerful in shaping the lives of people. All too often, we see horrible damage done to children and spouses because of the negative impact of what happens inside our families. But the reverse is also true. Those who come from great families where love is in abundance are also impacted, but in a good way. We all are in this impact group. We can all start with our own family and set our sights on creating great impact on the life of the people in our family.

What will be the size of your impact? Think big. Consider your capacity. Manage your resources. Now go for it!

Questions for Reflection:

Do you agree that it is just as easy to think big as it is to think small? Why or why not?

Would you describe yourself as a big thinker? Why?

Have you considered your capacity for impact?

Have you looked at the resources you can pull from to make your impact? What are they?

Do you execute? Or do you tend to procrastinate?

When you look at the scale of impact, where would you put yourself in terms of how big your impact would be?

Chapter Three

The Character and Skills of Impact

Do you remember earlier when I said that it requires both character and skill to make a long-term impact? Though the statement is true, I believe that character is far more important than your skills. Both are very important, but character is imperative, and I don't believe that we give enough attention to it in our modern-day world.

> **"Be more concerned with your character than your reputation, because your character is who you really are, while your reputation is merely who others think you are."**
>
> — John Wooden

Your character is who you really are. And, ultimately, your character will drive what you accomplish. So, before we get too far into this book, I feel it's important to remind us of the essential character traits that will help us achieve the impact we want to make in this world.

Integrity

In order to have a lasting impact in your life and business, you must have longevity. Of course, there are people who make a lasting impact in a short period of time, but typically it requires a good life or a good business over a long period. The more you can put those two things together, the more likely you are to leave a lasting impact.

The greatest way to ensure longevity is by embodying *integrity* in every area of your life and business. In fact, in my book *The Art of Influence* (and in my audio program by the same name), as well as my speeches, I talk about integrity a lot. I even go so far as to say that it is the foundation of influence, and influence is the key to lasting impact. Though there are all kinds of things required for success and influence, integrity is always number one.

I have always found the word integrity interesting. It's one of those words that everybody can spell and use correctly in a sentence, but I'm not so sure that people truly know what integrity is.

To help us understand what integrity truly is, let's take a look at the root word. Integrity shares the same root word as an old math term we learned in middle school—the integer. However, the tougher question is, what is an integer? Funny enough, I have asked this of over a million people in my speeches, and I've had less than 20 people raise their hand with the correct answer! An integer is a whole number. The root of the word integrity literally means "whole."

Now, looking at the root word, we can clearly see that to have integrity means to act out of wholeness. It means that you are complete, or perhaps an even better definition for what we are talking about here is *undivided*. To be undivided in your ways means that you hold to a single set of morals, ethics, and values.

Take a good long look in the mirror and ask yourself if you are acting out of integrity. To have integrity means you don't treat some people one way and other people another. It means you don't tell the truth on some occasions and lie on others. It means that you don't pay income tax on some of your income but hide the rest.

The problem for most people is that they don't understand how someone can judge whether or not we have integrity or not. But, here's the real problem. When someone else does something wrong, we look at them and we might think they lack integrity because of their actions. We judge their actions. On the other hand, when *we* do something wrong, we do not judge our actions; we judge our *intentions*.

The problem is that other people are judging our actions and not our intentions. That's the disconnect. We give ourselves a lot more grace than someone else would. In fact, when someone else does something wrong, what do we want? We want justice or compensation. But when we do something wrong, what do we want? Grace and forgiveness.

I have asked many people in my seminars if we have an integrity problem in America, and everybody agrees we do. Everybody raises their hands. Then, when I ask them how many of them would describe themselves as a person of little or no character, not a single hand goes up. In fact, no one has ever raised their hand. No one stands up and says that they're going to lie, cheat, and steal to succeed. Again, this is the disconnect. My audiences seem to say that yes, there's a problem, but don't think that they are part of it. That's when I began to dig in and realize that we don't understand how other people look at us.

In order to have a lasting impact, we need to maintain our integrity. Yes, of course, we all fail from time to time. We all break our own moral code. Whether you are a person of faith and call it sin, or a person who just calls our bad actions shortcomings, we can all agree that from time to time, people break their integrity.

If you want to have lasting impact, it is imperative that we not only live with integrity, but when we break our integrity, we quickly seek to make it right. In doing so, we will attract people and allow ourselves to make a more significant impact.

Excellence

If you want to leave a lasting impact, you will have to focus on excellence. Yes, I suppose you can leave an adverse lasting impact if you live the opposite of excellence, but that is not our goal. Our goal is impressive, lasting impact that makes life better for everyone around us.

I've had the great fortune of being able to travel the world, and one of my favorite cities is Florence, Italy. My bestselling book, *The Angel Inside*, is based in Florence, and I have since created wine and cooking tours that take people there to learn from my book and take in the amazing sights of Tuscany.

In the summer of 2019, on June 18th, my lovely wife, Denise, and I were married just outside of Florence, Italy, in a vineyard at a beautiful boutique hotel. It was an incredible day. Right after we were finished with the ceremony, Denise and my two stepdaughters, Angelina and Katelynn, had a driver take us into the city of Florence for a tour.

We were able to use my favorite tour guide, Ricardo, to take us through the museum where the David is and onto a quick tour of the city. It was on the tour after seeing the David that I learned something I had not known before. We stood before the doors of the baptistery, which is located right across from the main church in Florence. The Catholics didn't allow you to go into the church until you were Catholic, so they had you baptized into the faith in another building, after which you could then enter the church. The baptistery is incredible.

One of the most stunning things about the baptistery is the doors. There is one set that contains ten gold scenes from the Bible on them! The original doors are now in a museum elsewhere in Florence, but the replica doors are still astounding. Hundreds of people stand in front of those doors at any given moment. As we stood there, Ricardo asked us how long we thought it took the artist, Lorenzo Ghiberti, to create the doors before us. Now, as I thought, I figured it must have taken quite some time given how beautiful they are, but I would never have imagined how long it actually took. My guess was two or three years. I was really wrong!

Ricardo told us that it took Lorenzo 27 years to finish those two doors. He then asked us what we thought Lorenzo had done before those two doors. Incredibly, Lorenzo had also crafted the doors on the side of the baptistery, which took him 23 years. Think about that for a moment. 50 years. Five decades to make two sets of doors. Imagine, now, if you were someone in modern-day. You're in your seventies, and you look back over your life and the major accomplishment of your life was that you made two sets of doors. Most Americans would feel as though they had failed at life. It certainly wouldn't feel like you had made a lasting impact.

But then I started thinking about it. Five hundred years later, over two million people a year visit the city of Florence. Most of them stand before the doors that Lorenzo Ghiberti had made five centuries before. That is a lasting impact! (I want you to go to the internet and search for these doors. They are truly amazing.)

So, what made the lasting impact for Lorenzo? I believe it was his focus on excellence. Yes, he could have cranked out some lesser doors, but those doors would not have been placed in a place of prominence and seen by two million people a year.

What is the lesson for us in all of this? Focus on your excellence. No matter what your job, focus on doing it as well as you can. Commit yourself to doing every single thing in the best way possible. Doing things half-baked will never leave a lasting impact. Think of the books, songs, and movies that have made an impact on your life. They were all excellent. Think about the people that have made the biggest difference in your life. They were excellent. Excellence opens doors to impact.

Service

I have worked with some of the most extraordinary people in the world in my career, and it has been incredible. I've worked with leading politicians, world-class athletes, amazing business people, and many others who are making an impact in the world around them. In doing so, I've realized that most of them live a life that is, in one way or another, counterintuitive to what most of us think about successful people.

We often think that successful people got there by stepping on other people or cutting in line. We tend to think the world is run by those who dominate. Yes, of course, there are those people, and they are well known, but most of the successful people that I know and have worked with are quite the opposite! The people I work with are servants.

No, I don't mean that they work at a restaurant as a server. I don't mean that they are the butler. I mean that they are servants to those they work with and lead. They consider other people's interests as more important than their own.

My mentor, Zig Ziglar, has a famous quote where he says that you can have anything you want in life if you just help enough other people get what they want out of life. This is exactly what I've seen in the lives and businesses of people I have worked with. They serve other people first and foremost.

Isn't it interesting that on the famous McDonald's sign—the one outside of every one of their restaurants—there is a counter of how many people have been served? Not how many hamburgers have been made, not how many people have eaten there, but how many have been *served*. That is a great way of putting it, isn't it?

So, what does it mean to serve others? What does it mean to place their interests as more important than your own? Good questions. Let's dig in a little bit.

To serve others means that you will give of your time, effort, resources, and energy to engage with them; to help them for *their* benefit. You can be the leader of a company, perhaps even the sole owner, and you can still serve the people who work for you. It means that you set your sights on helping them before you help yourself. It's interesting when you see a business owner who is loved and adored by the people who work for them. It is almost always because that business owner loved, cared for, and served the people who worked for him or her.

Serving others means that you think of them first. You make your interactions about them and not you. I will give you a great example of how my daughter tripled her income with this principle.

When my daughter was 14 years old, she got a job as a barista at a coffee shop. It wasn't a Starbucks or big chain; it was a small, local coffee shop. She was paid minimum wage, which, at the time, I think, was about $9 an hour. But, I noticed something about her tips. When she first started working there, she would bring home about $25 a day in tips. Not bad for a 14-year-old girl. A few weeks later, she was regularly bringing home $50 a day in tips. Then, in about six weeks, she was regularly bringing home $75 a day in tips.

So, I called her into my office.

I asked her what was up, and she told me that she finally figured people out. I thought that was funny, and I asked her what she meant. She told me that she realized that people like to talk about themselves.

She told me that when she first started, she would just take people's orders and not talk to them. She would make their change and hand them their coffee. But then she realized she could start asking questions of people. So, she started with the regulars. Once she noticed that they were in there often, she would ask about their job and what they did. She asked about their college education, whether or not they were married, and asked about their children. She asked about their spouse's job. All she did was ask questions that allowed the person on the other side of the counter to talk about themselves.

She then explained that when she first started working there, she would make change for the customer, and a portion of the change went in the tip jar. Now, when she makes their change and talks to them, she said that all of the change goes in the tip jar!

There is an interesting truth there. Here were 40-year-old men and women being psychologically manipulated by a 14-year-old girl to feel good about themselves, thus giving her more money because of how they feel.

What is the truth we can pull out of here?

People long for someone to care for them. They want somebody to notice them. They want somebody to be interested in them. So much so that when a random, 14-year-old barista begins to ask them about their life, they feel so good they triple the amount of money they tip her.

Now, am I suggesting that we manipulate people in such a way? No, not at all. But I would say that it's something to recognize. We should recognize that we can make an impact on people simply by caring. It's attractive, and it creates loyalty. And, in order to make a big impact, you're going to need loyal people around you.

Are you willing to care for others? Are you willing to do for others? Are you willing to place other people's needs before your own? That is the way to have an impact.

Optimism

Optimism is imperative if you are going to make a lasting impact. Optimism is the fuel that drives ambition, success, and progress. If you think about it, nobody who has a negative assessment of the future is going to go there or try to take other people there.

Optimism is attractive to other people as well, which is important if you are going to make an impact on them. Everyone loves optimistic people. Yes, there are some who don't like people with the sunshine personality, but most do. The greatest leaders are those who are optimistic, who can paint the vision of the preferred future and move other people toward it.

I love to break down words, especially to the root. The way that I remember what optimism is, and a great way to define it is as follows.

First of all, the first three letters are "opt." What does it mean to opt? It means to choose. Optimism is a choice.

If you think about the first three letters and you apply them to the medical profession, what do you think of? An optometrist or an ophthalmologist, right? And what do these three things have to do with? How you see.

The way that I remember what optimism is, is this: We *choose* to see the world in the most positive way we can. It is a choice. Every situation has many ways you can look at it. You can look at things negatively, or you can look at things positively. For example, after 50 years of living in Seattle, I moved to Scottsdale, Arizona. Now, during the summer, Scottsdale can get very hot. One hundred fifteen degrees Fahrenheit is a regular occurrence in July and August. Most people down here complain about the heat. That is a negative perspective on the temperature. I take a more optimistic approach. I remind myself that I could still be living in Seattle, where we get ten months of rain. Now, I actually enjoy the heat.

Optimism is also about how you think. We are regularly rolling thoughts around inside of our heads, and our brains are constantly using words as we think. I don't think many people ever really give a whole lot of thought about the words that roll around inside their brains every day. But they should, because those words create attitudes, feelings, emotions, and, eventually, actions. Sitting around thinking negative thoughts produces negative actions.

Conversely, thinking positively produces positive states of mind, emotions, and, eventually, positive results. This is where we want to be. There's a Bible verse that says we should take every thought captive. I love that word imagery. It's almost as though we have negative criminal thoughts that run around in our brains, and we have to go arrest them and throw them in thought prison. We want to make sure that those negative thoughts aren't out on the streets, terrorizing people!

Another way that we demonstrate whether or not we are filled with optimism is through the words that we speak. In fact, if I listen to somebody talk for just 20 or 30 minutes, I can get a good idea as to whether or not they are an optimist or pessimist. It's all in how they perceive and project things.

We demonstrate our optimism from the surface-y things we say all the way down to the deepest thoughts we share. When people listen to you, they can also tell whether you are an optimist or a pessimist.

For example, what do you say when someone asks you how you are doing? Have you ever heard someone say something like, "I'm doing pretty good under the circumstances"? This is not optimistic at all. Who in the world wants to be under the circumstances? Furthermore, nobody wants to follow somebody who's under the circumstances! Nobody's going to look at you and say, "Oh, you're under the circumstances, can I come under there with you?" People who are going to help you make a big impact want to see that you can go over the circumstances, around the circumstances, or through the circumstances. Optimistic people know that they are not bound by the circumstances! They see a brighter future in spite of whatever it is they're going through.

Now, don't get me wrong; you don't have to be like a good friend of mine who is extremely optimistic. I called him up one time shortly after meeting him. When he answered, I asked, "How are you doing?" He said, "Chris, if I were any better, I'd have to be twins, and if I were somebody else, I'd be jealous of myself!" Now *that* is positive! He is one of the most optimistic people I've ever met. You, however, do not have to talk like that in order to be optimistic.

You just have to find your own unique personality. There is somewhere in between "If I were any better I'd have to be twins" and "Another day, another dollar" wherein you can demonstrate your own optimism through language that works for you. It has to be natural. Some of you reading are real introverts, and if you were to walk into the office next week sounding like a motivational speaker, people would think that you were on drugs. But there are some of you who are reading this who are very gregarious extroverts, and if you were to start expressing yourself in an overly optimistic way, people would just think it was natural. Either way, you have to find your own personality.

I would encourage you to listen to yourself speak for a couple of weeks and be honest with whether or not you are an optimist.

So, in order to make a lasting impact, you have to be optimistic. You have to control your thoughts and your words. You must also take optimistic actions. We must act in faith, believing that the outcome we hope for is going to happen.

For example, if you were thinking about starting a company, you would have to be optimistic about its chances of success. Eventually, the ultimate optimistic action is to actually start the business and throw the doors open for customers. But you have to believe in it. You have to work it out in your mind first. You have to proclaim it with your words to others. And then you must take action in order to produce the results.

Optimism is attractive to other people. The bigger your idea, the more people are going to want to help you make it a reality. So, whatever the lasting impact is that you want to make, view it with optimism, think big, proclaim it to others, take action, and see it come to fruition!

Optimism is about perspective—a *choice* of perspective. Any situation can be thought of or perceived in any way that we choose to. Successful people discipline themselves to choose the perspective that is the most optimistic.

Let me give you an example. Let's say that you are going to go to a small meeting with a few people you've never met before. There are two different perspectives you could take in how you could think about that meeting. One way you could think about it is that you probably won't like the meeting because the new people probably won't like you. Or, you could think of it another way, in that you could tell yourself that it is going to be exciting to meet some new people because you'll make new friends. In both of these perspectives, you still haven't even had the meeting yet. But you are choosing to think about the meeting in one way or the other. Frankly, you don't really know how the meeting is going to go, but it is likely to go better if you enter into it with a positive and optimistic attitude. And secondly, even if the meeting doesn't go amazingly, at least in the days or weeks leading up to the meeting, you won't be dreading the meeting and causing yourself a bad attitude.

Have you ever taken a look at how you choose your perspective on different things? Everything has the ability to be looked at in different ways, both negatively and positively. It is our job as people of impact to make ourselves into optimistic people so we can lead the way into a better place for others.

Perseverance

It may seem obvious, but in order to make an impact, you have to at least get to the end. And the only way you get to the end is to persevere. Why do you have to persevere? Because, as Jesus said, in this world, you will have trouble. It's true. Everything about life and business includes understanding that there are times of trouble and difficulty. We often run into roadblocks and obstacles. Unfortunately, most people quit when the going gets tough.

How will you ever know what the top of the mountain looks like if you stop before you get there? How will you ever know what is on the other side of the sea if, once you're halfway there, you turn around and come back? How will you ever know what your business could become if you decide to quit? How will you ever know what that relationship might turn out to be if you quit?

Now, don't get me wrong; there is a time to quit. But quitting is done all too often when what should actually happen is that you should continue. Most people quit at the first sign of difficulty. Successful people—people who make a lasting impact—are people who persevere and are tenacious.

World history is filled with stories of people who had to persevere through great trials in order to accomplish what they hoped to accomplish. People in business, people in other countries, and people in everyday situations succeed because they persevere.

What about you? Do you persevere? Or do you quit when the going gets tough? Remember the old book title from the famous minister, Robert Schuller? When the going gets tough, the tough get going. In order to be someone who makes an impact, you have to be tough, and you have to keep going.

> **"Nothing in this world can take the place of persistence. Talent will not; nothing is more common than unsuccessful people with talent. Genius will not; unrewarded genius is almost a proverb. Education will not; the world is full of educated derelicts. Persistence and determination**

alone are omnipotent. The slogan 'press on' has solved and always will solve the problems of the human race."

— Calvin Coolidge

I have worked with many successful people; people who have achieved the kinds of lives that make significant impact. I have also worked with many people who are not anywhere near doing so. Many times, those who are not successful resent those who are and believe that somehow success was handed to those who have achieved much.

What I have found, however, is that the reverse is true. Those who have made an impact have worked much harder than those who are not successful. You wouldn't believe the stories of struggle that I hear from those who now appear to be on "top of the heap."

Yes, they are successful, but no, it wasn't handed to them! They fought to make an impact. I find that most of the unsuccessful people who come to me actually haven't persevered at all. When I ask many of the people who complain about their lack of success why they haven't persevered, I usually get excuses. Yes, there are exceptions on both sides, but I find this to be almost universally true.

In fact, I recently had a coaching client who wanted help getting through his obstacles. I told him that I could help him in about three months, but he insisted on paying for twelve months. Why? Well, as he told me, he had regularly quit coaching programs before, and if he was going to commit, he knew he needed to commit to all of it. In his coaching, he really struggled. He told me what his problem was, and we began to look at what the possible solutions scenarios might be. One by one, he went through the list with an excuse as to why none of these options were really options. The only thing he left himself with was that he was stuck and had to stay in the same place he was currently in.

At the end of four out of his twelve months he committed to coaching, he sent me an email and told me that he was quitting. And he had already paid me! Years ago, I probably would have begged him to stay, but now I know those kinds of people. They are quitters. They always quit. They never make it through to the other side. It's unfortunate, too, because he is an obviously intelligent and skilled person. However, he's wrapped around the axle in so many areas of his life that he can't move forward, and he won't persevere or do the difficult work it takes to get through it. Thus, he stays right where he is.

If you are one who finds yourself dreaming of a better life, or looking at someone who "has it made," I would ask you to take a long, deep look inward at your life to find whether or not you have actually persevered in pursuit of your dreams.

How long have you gone for it? How many people who achieve much go for *years* before they achieve what their hearts long for? How hard have you gone for it? Most people who achieve much have sacrificed much. They strive valiantly for what it is that resides deep in their dreams. They just plain ol' work hard!

I have a friend, Eric Worre, who has always been pretty successful, but nothing extraordinary. He has always been an entrepreneur and has moved from building business after business. When I first met him, he was in the middle of a business he had raised some money to start but eventually collapsed and lost millions of dollars. Most people would quit and give up. Not Eric.

Instead, he created a YouTube channel. For years, he gave away free content and developed a database of followers in the seven figures. Then, he wrote his book and flipped the switch. People began to buy the book by the truckload. One day, at the very beginning of his big run, I was sitting on his back deck with him and asked him how many books a day he was selling. It was self-published, so he knew exactly how many books he was selling every day. He was averaging five thousand books a day. At an average profit of $10 a book, that's $50,000 a day!

He then started putting on conferences, and eventually got to the point where he was putting 10,000 to 20,000 people in a room all over the world four or five times a year. Now he has his own jet and just finished building a beautiful contemporary mansion with spectacular horizon to horizon views of the Las Vegas Strip. I don't know exactly how old he is, but I would guess he's somewhere right around my age, so in his early 50s. It was about 10 years ago that his business really took off, so in his early 40s. What would have happened if he would have quit in his late 30s? He would have never seen the impact he is making on millions of people worldwide. He persevered!

So, what are the principles of perseverance? Here are some thoughts to start your fire and get you going.

Sometimes you just have to outlast the others.

"Success seems to be largely a matter of hanging on after others have let go."

— William Feather

I have found that many people start on their dream of making an impact, but most never finish. Then, those who stop resent those who make it. The truth is, most people who become successful have simply mastered the art of keeping on keeping on!

I can remember early on in my career when I would get discouraged, and I literally said to myself, "One more week. Just give it one more week." Quite frankly, this is what got me through a couple of years of my work early on. I hung on as others let go. What if I would have quit? What if I wouldn't have persevered? You would not be holding this book in your hand. None of the other books that I've written that have been translated into 13 languages would have made the impact they're now making around the world.

It is easy to get disheartened. Ask those who have achieved success if they ever got disheartened, and you will find some of the most amazing stories you have ever heard. Give it a try: Go to the most successful person you know, somebody who's making a tremendous impact, and ask them if they ever thought about quitting. Ask them how they kept on going. You will be amazed at what you hear.

Sometimes you just have to hold on at the end.

> **"When you get to the end of your rope, tie a knot and hang on."**
>
> — Franklin Roosevelt

I wonder how many people have quit just as they would have begun their entrance into impact. Sure, there are many who quit at the first sign of hard work, but what about those who, after the tenth time of trial, give up, just as fate would have seen them go through one last hurdle and then into the promised land?

How many people were on their last hurdle and decided not to jump? How many people had just one more mountain pass to go? Or just one more river to cross?

Of course, we will never know, but certainly, some of the people who quit are doing so on what would have been their last trial, right?

So, what does this mean for you? For me, it means I do not quit because I would hate to find out later that all I needed was just one last effort, and I would have achieved my goal. What if it isn't my last trial? That's okay because as long as I keep going, eventually, I will get to my last trial, I will overcome it, and I will enter the Winner's Circle!

Sometimes the most beautiful results come from dull things under pressure.

> **"Diamonds are nothing more than chunks of coal that stuck to their jobs."**
>
> —Malcolm Forbes

If coal weren't an inanimate object, it would certainly scream, "Stop! I want out!" But that coal, when facing incredible pressure, is turned into one of the earth's most precious possessions. Ugly, dirty old coal is transformed into beautiful diamonds.

Instead of looking at pressure and trials as the reason to quit, persevere, and see them as the very thing that will make your life the beautiful thing that you desire it to be. See it as your opportunity to learn, to grow, and to be transformed. See these trials as the very things that will enable you to make your unique impact on the world around you!

Trials will surely come. Life will get hard. You will want to quit.

Then, you will have a choice: Will you give up? Or will you take your turn at tenacity? The choice you make will determine much of the rest of your life.

My advice? Persevere! You will become stronger, and you will end up making the impact on the world that you desire.

Transparency

The Dalai Lama says that a "lack of transparency results in distrust." The more we can reveal ourselves to people and allow them to see into us, the more they're going to trust us—if we are people of character. I think this is especially true in our day and age. We now have leaders who are very transparent, and transparency, along with authenticity, which I will be discussing in the next section, is being made more mainstream. We are tired of people hiding their true selves and wearing a mask that appears good from the outside, but underneath is a different story. The more you are willing to allow others to see through you to the real you, the more they are going to be attracted to you and will follow you on your road to impact.

Authenticity

What is it about authenticity that creates bonds between people? Well, think about something that is authentic. For example, a collector's item, perhaps a baseball card. Some baseball cards are worth millions of dollars... *If* there is a certificate of authenticity. What does that mean? It means that there is proof that it is real.

What does this mean for you? People want proof that *you* are real. They want to see the real you. They don't want to see a conjured-up vision of who you want them to think of you as. They want to see you, not an image of you. People who are authentic, those who are willing to let people see them for who they are, make the biggest impacts. I believe that it is our weaknesses and how we deal with them that allow us to get stronger, develop our character, and succeed. When other people see how we deal with our own weaknesses and faults, and we share how we overcome them, they are attracted to us and want to do business with us. Are you authentic? Do you allow others to see the real you? You should if you want to make an impact.

Vulnerability

Vulnerability has made a comeback in recent years. Brene Brown has been the one to most popularize the concept, challenging and encouraging people to embrace it. She began by giving a TED Talk on vulnerability, and it has since swept through the corporate world, earning Brene millions of dollars in contracts and speaking engagements and helping corporate people bring vulnerability into their work and leadership. I think this is a good thing. For far too long, people, especially leaders, thought they should never show vulnerability because they wanted to be strong for those they lead.

But people aren't looking for perfect leaders. They are looking for relatable leaders, and being relatable often comes down to knowing that though they might have extraordinary skills and character, he or she is also not perfect. If the leader is perfect, I have no hope because I know that I myself am not perfect! When the leader is vulnerable, it gives me hope because I know that I am weak as well, and impact is still an option.

I had a pastor tell me once that he never admitted any faults during a sermon because he wanted people to perceive him as a strong spiritual leader. He was young, probably under 30, and I told him that the exact opposite was true. If he was only a perfect spiritual leader for his congregation, or at least that was their perception of him, he would never make as much of an impact as he would if he let his congregation know of his struggles. Now, of course, I'm not talking about oversharing or telling a large group of people something that should be private information, but I am talking about letting people see a glimpse of what you struggle with. When they know that you struggle and still succeed, that gives them hope and they will follow along, helping you make your impact.

Thoughtfulness

George Herbert Walker Bush, the first George Bush to become president, the former vice president under Ronald Reagan, was renowned for his handwritten notes. He wrote tens of thousands of them over the course of his lifetime. In fact, his memoir is called *All the Best, George Bush: My Life in Letters and Other Writings*.

What did the senior Bush know about handwritten notes? He knew that they conveyed thoughtfulness. It meant that at some point, when he was away from another person, he was thinking about them. It means that he took time out of his day to make sure that his thoughts were conveyed to that other person. And that usually drew the other person even closer to President Bush. He wrote them to his family, he wrote them to his friends, he wrote them to all sorts of people, including his political enemies.

George HW Bush was one of the most successful politicians of the 20th century, and his history as an American citizen is one of service and impact to his country. I believe that his writing of notes was a major part of that because he gained support from people through his thoughtfulness.

If you think about it, handwritten notes are probably even more important now than they were in the late 20th century. Why? Because almost everything now is digital. People just send emails and texts. When was the last time you got a personal note from someone? Maybe it's been years. But when you did, how did it make you feel? Of course, it made you feel special! Why? Because we just don't get them very often.

I think another important thing about not only the thoughtfulness of notes in particular, but expressing thoughtfulness in general, is that it touches the heart of the other person. Simply sending a handwritten note is a sign of thoughtfulness, but there are varying degrees in which you can convey that thoughtfulness. The more we allow ourselves to be transparent, authentic, and vulnerable, the more our thoughtfulness comes through.

Do you take time to be thoughtful and to express that thoughtfulness to other people? If not, you're missing a big chance to make an impact on people. It can be as simple as writing a note. It can be leaving a voicemail. It can be sitting across from a friend or co-worker and looking them straight in the face and telling them how much you appreciate them. And the more specific you can be about what you appreciate, the more your thoughtfulness will come through. It may mean picking up a gift or running an errand for someone. Through it all, it means that you are thinking about the other person and a way to encourage or solve a problem for them. This creates impact!

I suppose there are many other character traits that I could go through, but I will leave these with you for now. I believe they are at the core of the character that we need to have in order to make the kind of impact that we want to leave on people and the world when we are gone.

Take a good long look in the proverbial mirror. Are you a man or woman of character? Be honest with yourself. We all have blind spots. In what ways can you become filled with more character? Make the growth of your character one of your key pursuits, and you will find yourself in a better place to make a bigger impact.

The Skills of Impact

On the other side of *character* are the *skills* required to make an impact. Those who excel in both their character and their skills are people who will find themselves making a tremendous impact on the people and the world around them.

I've been teaching character and skills for nearly 30 years, and one of the things that I have realized is that there are a lot more character traits to master for impact than there are skills. Having gone through so many of the character traits, I would like to focus on a few skills that are important as well.

Communication. I believe that communication is the single most important skill for life and business. If you think about it, everything we do all day long usually requires other people to be involved to one degree or another. This means that we have to take what is going on inside of us and somehow let other people know. That's the process of communication. Some people are very good at it, while most people find it difficult.

Even as a professional communicator who has made his living in the industry for over 30 years, I find communication difficult sometimes.

You would think that it would be pretty easy. I mean, I think it, I say it, you hear it, and we're done. But that's not the way that it works. It is far more difficult than that because of all of the things that go into communication. You have how you feel and think about what is going on inside of you. You have your ability to speak what you are thinking. You have all the circumstances taking place around you when you're talking. You have how well the other person hears it. You have how the other person thinks and feels about it. All of those things make communication much more difficult than we think that it should be. If you are going to make an impact, you should learn to communicate as best as you possibly can.

Vision-casting. This is similar to communication, and it involves communication, but it is very specific. This is about taking your vision for what you want to do and the impact that you want to make and the ability to clearly communicate that to others who can help you make that impact. You need to learn how to take that vision and help other people make it their own.

Team-building. Most of the impact you make is going to require the help of other people. You, as the leader, need to know how to bring other people around you and then how to get them to work together on the singular mission of making an impact around your vision.

Conflict resolution. This one may seem out of place, but the longer I live and the older I get, the more I realize that all of humanity is just one conflict after another. Even people who really like each other still end up in conflict. Of course, husbands and wives who pronounced endless love to one another at their wedding can still have a lot of conflict after they spend ten years together inside a 1,500-square-foot house. If that's the case, then there will undoubtedly be conflict among our team members. As the leader, we need to help people work together to create impact and be able to put aside their differences for the greater good.

I believe that anybody can make an impact, and they can, to a great degree, determine how significant that impact is. But first and foremost, they need to work on themselves. Growing your character and skills will go a long way toward helping you make the impact you want to make.

Take some time to go through this list of character traits and skills I have written about in this chapter. You can even come up with some of your own. But take a good long look in the mirror and do a self-analysis to determine how you feel you are doing in each area. Then, when you are done, think about how you can improve yourself in each of those areas. Doing so will put you on track for impact.

Questions for Reflection:

On a scale of 1 to 10, please rate yourself in the following areas:

Character Traits
Integrity
Excellence

Service
Optimism
Perseverance
Transparency
Authenticity
Vulnerability
Thoughtfulness

Skills
Communication
Vision-casting
Team-building
Conflict resolution

For those that you listed as a six or under, what can you do to improve in those areas?

Chapter Four

Dancing with Opportunity

Anybody can achieve anything. Do you believe that? I do.

But, there is a caveat that must be made. Those who become successful are those who walk through the door of opportunity when it swings open—that we know. But what is the secret to getting *through* the door of opportunity?

Being outside the door when it swings open.

A stagehand for Kenny G was in the auditorium with him one day, just the two of them, when the stagehand started to play Kenny's songs on the piano. Kenny didn't even know the guy could play the piano. Guess who became a keyboardist for Kenny G?

You see, you never know when the door of opportunity is going to open wide. For some, their big break comes early in life, and for others, it comes later. But, for everyone who has succeeded, there is one key similarity: They were ready. And for everyone who was ready, there were thousands more who weren't.

So, the principle is: Be ready! Are you ready? Here are some thoughts for you to consider to make sure you are.

Are your skills as sharp as they could be? Are they ready so that when your shot comes, you can perform?

Is your character deep enough to handle success? Let's face it: You don't want big success if your character isn't able to withstand it.

Are you working hard to position yourself now? While waiting for the door to open, your job should be developing your skills and character so that you can position yourself to get through the door before it closes.

Your door will open someday; it opens for everyone. It may only open once, or it may open many times. It's different for everyone, and life just isn't fair that way. But everybody gets a shot. Will you be ready?

When that huge door of opportunity opens up, will you be able to boldly walk through it?

Do everything you can to be ready. Don't just sit and wish and dream. Be proactive and make sure you are the most qualified when the door opens. Make sure you are the hardest worker. Make sure you are the closest to the door.

Sometimes opportunity just wants to dance with you, and when opportunity invites you to dance, you better know how to dance.

Kedon Slovis was the quarterback of the high school where two of my daughters go. We got to know him a little at some backyard BBQs. Great young kid. He was recruited by a few major colleges, including USC. He was considered a three-star recruit, which is good, but most quarterbacks going on scholarships to major college football programs are four- and five-star recruits. When he got to USC as a freshman, he was ranked fourth on the depth chart. For those of you who may not understand the terminology, that means he was expected to be fourth-string. In other words, Kedon wasn't playing anytime soon.

After spring and summer practices, Kedon ended up beating out two other quarterbacks and was positioned as the backup quarterback. In the first game of the year, the starting quarterback damaged his knee and was out for the season.

That meant Kedon was going to be the starting quarterback for the rest of the year for the USC Trojans.

To say that Kedon's first game went great would be a massive understatement. USC was not ranked, and they were playing a rival, Stanford, who was ranked 23rd in the nation. Kedon led the Trojans to a 45-20 win. More impressive than that was the fact that he broke the all-time record for yards passed at USC for a true freshman playing in his first game: 377 yards and three touchdowns.

The door of opportunity opened up, and opportunity was asking to dance. How did the season turn out for Kedon?

By the end of the year, Kedon had set the all-time records at USC in the following:

> Yards passing in a single quarter: 295
>
> Passing yards in a game: 515

Yards passing by a freshman: 3,242

400-yard games in a season: 4

Passes completed in a season by a freshman: 260

At the end of the season, Kedon was named Pac 12 Freshman Offensive Player of the Year. He was also named by the Football Writers Association of America to their first team of Freshman All-Americans. He is the first true freshman at USC to ever win freshman All-American honors.

Opportunity asked him to dance, and Kedon stepped onto the dance floor, well prepared.

I would like to tell you a little bit about his preparation and how a freshman can step onto that big-time stage and pull it off. Kedon had a secret weapon. His name is Kurt Warner.

If you're a sports fan, you already know who Warner is. But, for those of you who maybe don't, Kurt Warner is a Hall of Fame, Super Bowl-winning quarterback. In retirement, he was an assistant coach for a local high school football team. Guess whose football team? That's right, Kurt Warner was Kedon Slovis' high school quarterback coach.

I believe that having Warner as his coach was a major part of what set Kedon apart. In fact, running the college football playbook was actually easier than the one they ran in high school because Warner ran such an advanced offense. Now, to get an understanding of this, you have to understand just how complicated a professional NFL playbook is. And this is what they were running in high school! It was very easy for him to step out onto that field and be advanced over his peers because, in many ways, he was playing something more simple.

In order to demonstrate to you how difficult an NFL play is, I reached out to my friend JJ Birden, who was an incredible wide receiver in the NFL, and I asked him to give me a typical play that might happen in an NFL huddle. This is what he wrote me back:

This is what the quarterback would say: "200 Wing Left Zip, 2 Jet Dallas Y H cross, X post, Z In."

This is what the quarterback would mean:

1. 200 tells the offensive line the blocking protection.
2. Wing tells the RB where to line up; left side off the tackle.
3. Zip tells the Z receiver to motion in then go back out.
4. 2 Jet Dallas is the pass play, so Y runs a middle seam route, and then H comes off his tail running a 6-yard shallow cross.
5. X runs a go to clear it out for the TE, who is the number one read while Z runs an 18 yard in route.

If they blitz on a side where we don't have enough guys to block it, all this goes out the window, and everyone runs their hot route, which is a short quick route so the QB can get it out fast. We have to watch all of this and be on the same page as the QB.

Or, if the QB thinks we can get in a better play, he calls an audible. In the huddle, we know the live color.

So, if he says Black Razor, he's changing the play, and everyone knows what their responsibility is on the Razor route.

There's a lot to process on every single play. This is one of the difference makers as to who makes it and who doesn't. All the NFL players must have the ability to process the information on the fly, under pressure, and execute at a high level consistently.

Do you understand any of that? I only understood a little bit of it! It makes the point, though, that this, being a typical play, can be difficult to understand. Kedon's preparation in high school is what led him to excel in college. He was prepared. And he was prepared by his mentor, Kurt Warner.

A lot of people would find themselves in that situation and not be able to perform. Whether in sports or in business, oftentimes opportunity asks us to dance, and all we can say is, "I'm sorry, but I don't know how to dance."

Impact makers know how to dance!

I have gotten what a few people would consider lucky breaks. I don't consider them lucky at all. Doors of opportunity were certainly open to me, but *I* was the one who was prepared. And I could dance!

When John Maxwell's team called to ask me to ghostwrite for him, I was prepared. I was an excellent writer, and I knew Maxwell's material well. After almost two years of writing for

Maxwell, I received a call from Jim Rohn and his team. They wanted me to come and work with Jim and write some learning programs with them. I was prepared and able to do that.

If I wasn't a good writer or didn't know the topics that Jim spoke and wrote about, or if I didn't have the discipline to write regularly so as to create the one-year learning program we created, the open door of opportunity would have been for naught.

What are you doing to prepare yourself for when opportunity opens the door and asks you to dance?

When it opens, be ready!

Questions for Reflection:

If a big opportunity came your way for you to make an impact, would you be ready right now?

If you are not ready for opportunity now, what do you need to work on to prepare yourself?

Chapter Five

Overcoming Obstacles and Failure

The difference between the successful and unsuccessful is not the absence of obstacles, but the presence of perseverance.

Most people think that those who become successful had an easy time of it, or they were born with a golden spoon in their mouth, but this simply isn't true. I've worked with high achievers for 30-plus years, and the one thing I know to be true almost universally is that they've had rough lives and have had to persevere to overcome obstacles and get past failure.

Everyone faces obstacles. Everyone has had—and will continue to have—failure. If you want to have an impact on this world, you need to accept that and deal with it appropriately.

Obstacles come in many forms. Those obstacles can be your own shortcomings, a lack of money, people who disappoint you or take advantage of you, sickness, and all sorts of other things. These things happen to people who are successful, and these things happen to people who are unsuccessful. One of the things that makes people successful, however, is they learn how to deal with obstacles and failures.

People who don't make an impact quit when the going gets tough. That's why they don't make an impact. When they face an obstacle, they stop. Successful people—people who make an impact on the world—face their obstacles and figure out a way to go over them, around them, under them, or through them!

Remember my chapter on character and skills? This is very appropriate for getting through obstacles. It's going to take character. You're going to have to dig down deep and face those obstacles head-on. You're going to have to have skill sets that allow you to overcome those obstacles. Perhaps this is why so many people are stopped in their tracks when they face an obstacle. They don't have the character to push them through, or the skill sets to navigate the obstacles.

And failure... Most people think that failure is final. As it has been said, failure is neither final nor fatal. Failure can actually be a great gift. Most of the people that I know who have experienced great success and impact have had at least one major failure in their past.

Failure is an amazing teacher. You can learn all sorts of things about yourself and the world around you by your failure. Some of the greatest business leaders of all time experienced significant failures. In fact, just Google the term "great business leaders who have experienced failure," and you will see article after article listing some of the greatest names of modern history, including Bill Gates, Steve Jobs, Colonel Sanders, and Thomas Edison!

What each of them experienced was the learning cycle of failure. Thomas Edison is famous for saying that every time he failed, it was just one more way he knew not to do it in the future.

"You may have to fight a battle more than once to win it."

—Margaret Thatcher

Failure. Even the word sounds bad, doesn't it? That's because, since the time we were just young children, we were taught that failure was bad. But is that true? Is failure bad? Let's consider some things.

I like a good baseball analogy. Do you know who set the record for a season batting average (meaning how many times the batter successfully hit to get on base)? It is a gentleman by the name of Ted Williams, and his season batting average was .406 in 1941. That means that out of 1,000 times at bat, he would get a hit 406 times. That is considered by baseball fans as one of the greatest records ever. There are players making millions of dollars who hit .280!

But what does that stat also tell us if we flip it around? It tells us that the best season any batter ever had in the major leagues was a failure rate of .594. Even the best fail on a regular basis!

What about the richest people on Wall Street? Do they fail? Of course, they do. They pick bad stocks sometimes, but they cut their losses and learn from their failures.

Did Michael Jordan miss shots? More than 50 percent of them!

So, what about all this? What does this mean for us? The fact is, I think we can learn a lot about failure that will actually make us a great success. Here are some thoughts to help you use failure to further your future.

Failure is inevitable if you are trying for greatness. Failure is something we must accept as a part of the road we travel to success. This is a very important item, and it's number one on the list because a lot of what stops people from pursuing success is the fear that they may fail and not reach their destination. When we embrace the fact that we *will* fail, and that is okay, then we have nothing to fear anymore. Instead, we keep our eyes open and pick ourselves up, adjust to the failure, and move on.

Failure is never failure unless you fail to learn something from it. That's right; we ought to stop calling these bumps in the road "failures" and start calling them "learning experiences!" When you fail, the first thing you should think is, "What can I learn from this?" If you can pull just one idea out of that question, then the experience was worth it.

Sometimes, failure is a blessing in disguise. Just ask 3M. Engineers there were looking for an incredible adhesive and actually got a sticky paste that held, but not permanently. What a failure! No, instead, they spread some on the back of little sheets of yellow paper and called them "Post-It Notes." Have some? I'm sure you do. 3M thanks you for rewarding its "failure."

People won't think poorly of you if you fail. This is perhaps the biggest myth, and it's the one that causes us to never attempt our dreams. We don't try because of what Aunt Martha may say about us at the family reunion. The truth is, however, people will actually respect you for trying. The only thing I have found that causes people to think poorly about you is if you handle yourself badly when you fail. Sore losers get the bad press, not people who attempt great things!

Failure isn't the end, but the beginning. One of our greatest fears is that our whole world will collapse if we fail—or at least the project will. The truth is, that rarely happens! Most of the time, we can pick back up again, make some adjustments, and be on our way. This is a new beginning. Now, there is no need to go down the road you have already taken, so there is one less option you have to try on your new journey.

Sometimes we miss out on success because we quit in the middle of a problem. When we do so, it becomes a failure instead of an obstacle we could have persevered through. When people encounter trouble, they have a tendency to quit and then see themselves as having failed. My question is this: What if they would have kept on going—if they had persevered? Perhaps they would have struggled a bit and then broken free again. The failure happened only because they quit! So, don't give up. Keep pushing, and perhaps you will see yourself through to victory!

The greatest thing to overcome is the fear of failure. Most of the battle is right between our ears. It has been said that, "We have nothing to fear but fear itself," and that is true because in most of our "failures," the end result is usually much less scary than we feared it would be. Yet, in giving in to fear and not trying, we suffer the ultimate consequence: No success! So, begin to tell yourself the good stuff. Change the direction of your thinking and begin to see the possibilities of success, not failure.

The key is to understand that obstacles and failure are part of successfully making an impact!

Questions for Reflection:

How do you typically respond to obstacles? Do you shrink back, or do you push through?

What obstacles are you facing right now that could actually be opportunities?

How do you typically respond to failure?

What failures have you had in the past that, in hindsight, you realize were making you stronger and preparing you for the future?

Chapter Six

The Powerful Impact of Relationships

The best thing about life? People. The worst thing about life? Also people. Relationships with people are the deepest, most fun, and fulfilling thing about life. When they are working, life is grand. Relationships are also the most frustrating, hurtful thing about life. The key is to make sure that we get those relationships *right!*

Relationships are at the very core of our existence, and something we deal with every day and on every level of our lives. We have very superficial relationships with many people, such as merchants we meet, and relationships that we consider intimate, such as the ones we experience with our immediate family and our spouses.

Relationships provide us with both the most positive as well as the most negative experiences we have in our lives. There are those who, though they may never achieve fame or fortune in this world, will be remembered very highly by all who came in contact with them. Their funerals will overflow with people they have touched. They will have had *impact!*

The pain and joy that can come as children remember their deceased parents is determined by the lives those parents lived and how well they maintained the relationships with their children.

I believe that your impact comes down to the ability to maintain healthy relationships. Get that right, and you are well on your way to impact!

Think about the people who have a lifelong impact on you because of your relationship with them. I can think of a few:

Ms. Canafax, my 3rd-grade teacher who allowed this unruly little kid to be himself.

Sam Samuelson, my youth minister in high school. He told me about God and kicked me in the butt when I needed it.

Dr. Don Douglas, my college professor who asked this rough-around-the-edges young man to lead our college ministry to Seattle homeless people every Saturday night.

Mike Murphy, president of Mars Candies, one of the largest and most successful companies in the world, who was an early mentor of mine and supporter of my work.

Kyle Wilson, president of Jim Rohn International, who gave me a big break by bringing me in to work with Jim Rohn.

Zig Ziglar, who I co-hosted a television show with, *True Performance*, and who I always admired.

Jim Rohn, who allowed me into his world and endorsed my work to others.

Kevin Mather, one of my closest friends and president of the Seattle Mariners, who has been with me through thick and thin, given me advice, and was always there to challenge and encourage me.

Bryan Heathman, my publisher, and friend. His work on my behalf to get my books and audio programs out to the world so I can make my impact is invaluable. He and his wife DeeDee are close and cherished friends of Denise and mine.

Larry Winget, best-selling author and legendary speaker who became a friend of mine later on in life when I was coming off the worst ten years of my life. His friendship and advice were crucial at that time of my life, and it has become a great partnership.

Denise, my wife. It's hard to know where to even begin. Denise is my ultimate supporter!

All of these people have made a significant impact on me, and their support has helped me, in turn, impact millions of people through my work. Their belief in me gave me wings to fly.

I want to share with you the key components of establishing relationships that will allow you to leave a fantastic relational legacy and make the most impact that you possibly can.

Be Purposeful. People are busy, and time flies. Put these two together, and you have a recipe for disaster in the relationship department. Pretty soon, you and your best friends have had months go by between times spent together. In order to have quality relationships, we have to be purposeful.

This is especially true with couples, and even more so for couples with small children. They need to be very purposeful in making sure they spend quality time together, communicating and enjoying one another. Setting and keeping a date night will help you impact your spouse. Making sure that you spend quality time with your children will create impact. Making sure that you have healthy relationships with others, in general, will impact them significantly.

Be Proactive. This is the opposite of being *reactive*. Reactive is when your spouse says, "We never spend any time together," and you respond by saying, "Okay, we will this week." Proactive would be to sit down at the beginning of each month or week and schedule the time, or better yet, have a weekly "date night." The key is to take control and schedule your relationships. Otherwise, they are going to get away from you, and that will have a negative effect on your impact.

Be Disciplined. Yes, it takes discipline to maintain healthy relationships. The discipline is to make investments regularly. This means the monthly lunch with a friend. It means the yearly hunting trip with the guys from high school. It means cutting out of work early to go to your child's game. It means disciplining yourself to work harder during the day in order to leave at a set time so you can eat dinner with your family. All of these are acts of discipline. Just as we have to discipline ourselves in other areas of our lives, like exercising for health or investing for wealth, we have to discipline ourselves into actions that will produce strong and healthy relationships.

Value People Above Possessions, Schedules, and Achievements. The sooner we realize that we leave behind all of our stuff when we die, the sooner we will be able to focus on what matters most—relationships. Don't get me wrong; I am not saying that we shouldn't do our best to become successful financially or that we shouldn't enjoy material possessions. What I am saying is that it should be secondary to healthy relationships. I can't imagine someone on their deathbed who says, "I wish I would have left an estate of ten million dollars instead of five million." No, people get to the end of their lives and wish they would have invested more in their relationships.

Be Loving. I don't mean to be guided by emotional feelings of "love." Feelings come and go. This is what I mean when I say loving: To always act in such a way as to do what is best for the other person. Love is not feelings, but actions. When we say that we love someone, we mean that we are committed to their best interests. If we are lucky, those commitments are coupled with strong emotional bonds as well.

Be Forgiving. The fact is this: Where there are people, mistakes will be made. I don't care if you are the nicest guy on earth (or married to him), you will have some breakdowns in your relationship on occasion. That is the nature of being human. Other people will fail you, and you will fail other people.

When this happens, we must face a decision: Will we let the relationship remain broken, or will we learn to forgive? An analogy might be in order here. A relationship is like building a house. It has to have a strong foundation. That is where you start. Then, it must be built step by step until it is finished. During the building process, there may be times when a beam falls, or the two-by-fours break. The builder has a decision to make. Will he repair the building, or let it go? If he chooses to let it go, the house will be weak and eventually fall into disrepair. Unfortunately, too many people let their relationships break and do not repair them by practicing forgiveness. People who leave successful relationships behind them practice the art of forgiveness. Forgiveness keeps you on the road to impact. In fact, for some, the act of forgiveness will literally be the impact. Some people will remember you forever *because* you forgave them.

Follow the Golden Rule. I had a friend once who told me that he believed in the "Golden Rule." Now, he wasn't the most religious guy I knew, so I was surprised that he even knew the Golden Rule. I asked him what it was, and he replied, "He who has the gold, makes the rules." He was serious. Swing and a miss!

The golden rule of life is, "Do to others what you would want them to do to you." What is most interesting about this is that Christ was the first religious leader to say this in a positive way. Other leaders had said before to "Don't do to others what you don't want them to do to you." Relationships are about being proactive and doing for others. Make it your goal to be proactive in the way you treat others.

When we wake up each day with the goal to follow the Golden Rule and do good in people's lives, we set ourselves on a course that will allow us to build a strong relational legacy.

Think of how you want to be remembered, and then live in such a way that you will be. If you want to be remembered as kind, be kind. If you want to be remembered as strong, be strong. If you want to be remembered as friendly, be friendly. If you want to be remembered as forgiving and patient, be forgiving and patient. What you do and how you act will add up to how you will be remembered.

I wrote an article years ago that I want to share with you in this chapter about relationships because relationships are incredibly important.

Z.I.P.

Relationships are really what makes the world go 'round, aren't they? I mean, good, positive, healthy, and meaningful relationships provide us with the richest experiences we have here on this old earth of ours. Your loving spouse who shares everything with you; the best friend who connects with you like few others do; the people at work who appreciate you and help you to become the best that you can be. This is what brings joy to life!

But… relationships can also be the bane of our existence! What really brings more pain in this life than a broken relationship, especially when it isn't just broken but downright ugly? So, it behooves us to do all that we can to keep our relationships zipping right along, doesn't it? If we put our very best into our relationships, we can almost guarantee getting the very best out of our relationships!

Through the years, I have spent hundreds of hours working with people in their relationships: Marriages, friendships, working relationships, and social relationships. Through it all, I have seen some wonderful things and some terrible things. It truly is the good, the bad, and the ugly! But, I have been able to find three core elements of successful relationships. These are things that, when done over time, begin to create for you the kinds of relationships that you truly desire. They are the kinds of relationships you have always dreamed of.

The key to remembering these three items is the acronym Z.I.P.

Z.I.P. stands for three things you can do—and begin to do immediately—to improve any of your relationships. They are:

- Put some ZEST into your relationships.
- Cultivate more INTIMACY in your relationships.
- Develop a PURPOSE in your relationships.

Let's take a closer look at each of these three.

Put some ZEST into your relationships.

By zest, I primarily mean fun. Relationships were meant to be fun! We wouldn't have been made with the capacity to have fun if relationships weren't supposed to have a little zest in them.

Think about it: Don't you usually start out most healthy relationships with a lot of fun times? Whether it is going out to dinner or a ballgame, spending time playing a board game, or even just a lively talk, you usually have fun as a major part of the relationship. Fun is some of the glue that bonds the relationship.

But, as life goes on—specifically in a marriage, but in all relationships, really—the fun starts to go by the wayside. More and more, it is about getting the job done—whatever the "job" may be.

To restore the relationship, to put a little zip into it, we need to reintroduce the idea of zest.

What about you? Have you lost the zest? What can you do to get it back? Think of a specific relationship you have: What were the fun things you did at the beginning of the relationship that acted as the glue that bonded you together? Now, commit to doing those and see if your relationship doesn't begin to soar again. If you can, develop new fun things to do together so you can both start an adventure of fun with one another!

Cultivate more INTIMACY in your relationships.

First, a couple of clarifications: One, I don't just mean intimacy in the currently common understanding that is sexual intimacy. I mean, for all intents and purposes, taking your relationship to a deeper level. Second, I don't mean that you have to start doing group hugs with your workmates or having revelation sessions where the tissues flow freely.

What I do mean is that every relationship that is mutually satisfying has a level of depth to it that provides meaning. This is really what the search is for in our relationships: *meaning*.

Remember when you first started your relationship, whether with your spouse or friend? All of that time was likely spent opening up, sharing who you are, where you are from, what your likes and dislikes are. There was a deep sense of satisfaction with the relationship—that is why it continued. You liked who they were, and you enjoyed being known by them.

But then, something happens. We get to a certain level, and the pursuit of depth ends. We stop sharing feelings, likes, and dislikes. We stop sharing joys and dreams and fears. Instead, we settle into a routine. The daily grind takes over, and we stop knowing one another and simply exist together. Now, don't get me wrong; every time you get together doesn't have to be deep.

Remember, I am the one who advocates in the previous paragraphs for just having plain old fun sometimes. But, there is a need for regular times of intimate connection where we go deeper with others.

This is particularly hard for many of the male species like myself; however, it is not only possible, but healthy and needed! If we want to have the kinds of relationships we were made to have, we have to open ourselves up to having others know us, and for us to know others.

True meaningful relationships come when we are loved and accepted for who we are at our core, not for simply acting the right way in our relationships to keep the other person in it.

Think about the relationships you would like to see improvement in. Take some time in the coming weeks and months to spend time just talking and getting to a deeper level in your relationship. Specifically, let the other person deeper into your world. You can't force the other person to be more intimate, and you certainly can't say, "Let's get together and have an intimate conversation," because that would be too contrived. But you *can* make a decision for yourself that you will let others into your world. Perhaps this will be the catalyst for them doing the same.

You can guard yourself against intimacy, but you won't go much deeper, and you will feel a longing in your heart for more. Or, you can begin the deepening process and see your relationships change for the better.

Develop a PURPOSE in your relationships.

The most meaningful relationships we have are those that are held together by a common purpose and vision for what the relationship can accomplish, not only for those involved, but also for a greater good. Let's face it: When people have a common purpose, they feel like they are part of a team and feel bound together in that relationship. Even when people may be disappointed in the person they are in relationship with; if they have a purpose, such as raising the children, they are much more likely to stick it out. Purpose creates bonds.

So, what happens if we are proactively involved in seeking out a common purpose with those who we want to have a relationship with or those who we already have a relationship with, but would like to see it go deeper? Well, it gets better and stronger.

Think about your strongest relationships. Aren't they centered around at least one area of purpose or a common goal?

What about a relationship that has cooled? Think back and see if perhaps you used to have a common purpose, but it has since gone by the wayside.

And what of your desire to see a relationship grow? Take some time to begin to cultivate a common purpose. Sit down with that person and tell them that you would like to have some common goals; some purposes that you pursue together. As you develop these, you will see your relationship strengthen in ways you never imagined!

Let's recap: You want your relationships to show a little "zip?" Then put a little Z.I.P. in them:

- Put some ZEST into your relationships
- Cultivate more INTIMACY in your relationships
- Develop a PURPOSE in your relationships

Marriage

Lastly, on relationships, I feel compelled to talk about your marriage relationship since, for better or worse, you will have the most impact in your life on your spouse.

Research has proven that those who are happy at home are more productive and less stressed at work. Developing a better relationship with your mate can help you develop a better life, a better business, and that results in greater impact! Here are some thoughts to chew on for developing a strong and healthy relationship with your mate.

Listen. Communication is the key to a lasting relationship, and listening is the key to communicating. Too often, when we are quiet, we are not listening but waiting to speak. Instead of listening to what our mate is saying and intently trying to understand them, very often, we are making mental notes of what we would like to say in response. This is particularly true for us men. We often are trying to find the weakness in our mate's argument rather than really listening to the words that they're saying and the manner in which they're saying it. Why not take some time this week trying to internalize and understand your mate's words and feelings?

Schedule a regular time to go out or spend time together. With today's busy lifestyles, it is too easy to put our relationships on the back burner and take them for granted. While we might have every intention of spending regular time with our mate, we often find ourselves driven by a schedule that has us running in every direction and leaving us little time for our most important relationships. Work gets in the way. The kids get in the way. Our hobbies get in the way.

We need to realize the value and importance of that relationship with our mate and its effect on our whole life. Then we need to make spending time with our mate a major priority by scheduling a specific time at least once a week to get alone together, talk, and simply renew our relationship. Be sure to set some time aside each week to rediscover each other and enjoy your time together. Pencil it into your schedule, and don't give up that spot. In fact, it is probably best if you and your mate sit down and decide what night will work each and every week, then put it into your calendar. If someone asks you if you're available at that time, you tell them you already have an appointment. In the long run, that time that you spend with your mate will help you to become more of a success than you could ever fathom.

Consider your mate's interests more important than your own. When each person has decided to give of themselves to the other, you form a reciprocating relationship of love, concern, and devotion. When you come to a place where you disagree or where the two of you have differing opinions, try to get to the point where you can consider what your mate likes as more important than what you would like to do. The simple decision to do this goes a long way toward developing a healthy relationship!

Learn your mate's love language. There is a lot of talk recently about love languages. What this is, is that each individual has certain ways they receive love from other people. Some people like to have time spent with them. Others like gifts, small or large. Still, others respond best to physical touch. And others appreciate verbal affirmation. Our tendency is to show love the way that we like to receive love, but what will recharge our relationship fastest is to find out what way our mate likes to receive affirmations of our love. So, next time you get a chance to speak to your mate, ask them which of the above ways they like best to receive your demonstration of love. Then make a conscious effort to begin showing your love to them in that manner.

Do the small things you did when you first fell in love with your mate. Do you remember when you were first in love? Remember the small things you did to show your affection to your mate? But, as time went along, you probably began to get weighed down with simply living life and forgot the small things that made the difference in the beginning. Things like a phone call in the middle of the day just to talk or say, "I love you," an appreciative note, flowers, gifts, or opening doors. Recharge your relationship by consciously going back and doing the small things that you did when your love first began to grow.

Forgive. I've done a lot of work with couples who were having troubles, and one of the most common elements I find that is working against the development of their relationship is that they are holding something against the other and aren't willing to forgive. The fact is, your mate is going to fail you from time to time. We need to understand that. What we do when we get to that point, however, is what will make all the difference in the world. In a relationship that is going to last, the people involved are committed to forgiving one another. Those whose relationships last longest, and will be the healthiest, are those who are committed to forgiveness.

It is possible to leave a wonderful relational legacy and have a tremendous impact. If you follow these principles, you will surely do so.

Questions for Reflection:

How would you rate yourself in regard to your ability to create mutually beneficial relationships?

How do you feel about the statement that relationships are both the best and the worst things about life?

When you think about the relationships in your life that have had the most impact on you, who would you put on that list?

Do you know your purpose in relationships?

Are you proactive about building your relationships? How so?

Do you follow the Golden Rule when thinking of your relationships? How so?

When you think of the Z.I.P. Theory—zest, intimacy, and purpose—how do you rate yourself?

Do you find it easy or difficult to listen to others?

Do you and your spouse have a regularly scheduled date night?

Are you aware of your mate's love language?

How easy is it for you to forgive?

Chapter Seven

Impact the Impactors

Sometimes, you influence a greater group of people by influencing what I call *influencers*. I learned two great lessons about this from two legendary men I have had the great fortune of working with. One is John Maxwell, and the other is Jim Rohn.

John Maxwell tells a story of when he was a young pastor and couldn't get the church board to agree to do some things that he wanted to do. They just didn't seem to listen to him. Then, he realized that the most powerful man on the church board— who everyone listened to—was somebody he should spend some more time with. This man got the rest of the board to agree to John's ideas.

The man was a farmer, so John began to go out to his house and help him with some work once a week. While he was there, he would make suggestions to this man about things that could be done to improve the church. When the man seemed open to those ideas, John would ask him if he would bring them up to the board. John found that he was able to get a lot more done when the man with the influence spoke about them than when he did himself. That's a great lesson on how to influence people who are influencers!

Another story that showed me the profound impact that influencing influencers can have on the world was in 2004, at the annual meeting of the National Speakers Association. The outgoing president that year, who was celebrating the end of his year by overseeing the annual conference, was a good friend of mine, Mark Sanborn. The president of the National Speakers Association is given the authority to give away an award called "The Master of Influence." These are given to speakers who have made a tremendous impact on the world around them. In 2004, Mark decided to give the award to Jim Rohn. I sat next to Jim at that dinner and saw firsthand the impact he has had on so many people, including myself.

While Mark was making his introduction of Jim for the award, he asked the nearly 2,000 speakers in attendance if they would raise their hand if Jim Rohn had a significant impact on their life and speaking business. It was incredible to turn and look at the crowd with Jim and see nearly three-quarters of them raising their hands.

Of course, Jim has spoken to millions of people over the course of his lifetime. In fact, the last year that he spoke regularly, which was two years before he died, Jim spoke in 27 countries. He was well into his 70s when he did this. He obviously had an amazing impact on the audiences who heard him speak. But then, I started doing the math...

If 1,500 speakers give 30 speeches a year to an average of even 500 people at each event, that means over 22 million people are affected and influenced each and every year by people who Jim Rohn influenced. This is the ripple effect. Then, those 22 million people take what they learn from those 1,500 speakers and apply it to their own lives and even teach others, causing the ripple effect to go even further. Who knows where Rohn's influence will actually end once it gets a few places removed!

These two stories have made me acutely aware of my own desire to influence influencers. I lead high-level masterminds with successful people who do business all over the world. By leading these folks and challenging and encouraging them, I not only impact them, but I impact the people *they* impact.

Let me ask you, who do you impact? And who do you impact that impacts others? Know that, in the grand scheme of things, it isn't just the people who you impact, but the people they impact (and so on) that create your lasting legacy. This is one of the reasons I like writing books, because these books will exist long after I have passed away. And the people who read my books will go and influence others.

Make a commitment to influence everyone around you, yes, but be sure to have a strategy for influencing people who influence others. In doing so, you make your own lasting impact even bigger.

Questions for Reflection:

Who are the influencers you could impact to grow your influence and impact?

How can you create relationships with them to maximize your impact?

Chapter Eight

Personal Impact - Family

One of the most overlooked places we all have an impact on is our family. Particularly, our children. Too many parents are running around trying to change the world when they should be focusing on developing their children. This is a place where you can have maximum impact.

I confess that I didn't have much of a role model when it came to the kind of impact a parent could have. I often say that my mother was both the best and worst thing that ever happened to me. On one hand, she taught me that I could do anything that I wanted to, which made me very ambitious. But, on the other hand, she was extremely negative and verbally and physically abusive, which created harm in my life that took years to get over.

I know that if you're reading this, you want to have a tremendous impact on your children. And you can! However, I do think that it requires thoughtfulness and discipline to make sure we do what it takes to have an impact on our children.

I have a good friend, Todd Stottlemyre, whose story is particularly inspiring because of the impact that his dad had on him, and he now has on his children.

You may be familiar with the name Mel Stottlemyre. He is a Hall of Fame New York Yankee who played on some of the best teams the Yankees ever produced. He was teammates with legends like Mickey Mantle. Mel even has his own statue at Yankee Stadium. Now, *that* is legendary!

For this chapter, I reached out to Todd to ask him what it was like to grow up with a father who was a legendary player on one of the five greatest franchises in sports history in the biggest media market in the United States. What Todd wrote was both eye-opening and heartwarming. Here's what Todd says about growing up with his dad and the lessons that he learned.

> "Our dad taught us a lot of great lessons. One of the biggest lessons I learned from my dad was not to let other people's opinions have an effect on us. You can imagine being a professional athlete in the New York City media market, that there were all sorts of opinions about my dad and the other players. But he never let it affect him. He taught us the same thing, and that has been a powerful lesson for us.
>
> "We grew up around legends in what they call 'the House That Ruth Built.' We called it the School of Champions. The people that I got to meet made a profound impact on me as a young man.

"My dad was an incredible human being. He wasn't perfect, of course, but he was an amazing father. Even when I failed in many ways in my life, I always had a point to go back to. He was a set point for me that allowed me to know what the standard was—a standard that I live now for my children.

"The day that my father died, it was all over the news. They interviewed teammates, managers, and owners, and the one thing that was amazing was that they all talked about Mel Stottlemyre the *person*, not the ballplayer.

"People love to look up to my father as a person, but what we knew as his family was that he was ten times the person privately as he was publicly. Even in fighting the war of cancer, he always made sure that everyone else felt better. He was always thinking of other people. It made me want to always ask about how I can leave other people better.

"The biggest lesson that my father taught me was to ask the question, 'Is this the best that I can do?' Whether it be in my role as a dad, husband, brother, friend, or business person, I want to always be the best version of myself that I can, and I learned that from my father, Hall of Fame New York Yankee— who was even more so a Hall of Fame father."

What a great legacy. So, how can we make the same kind of impact?

Well, first of all, we have to *be right* in order to *teach right*. The best thing you can do for your children is to be the best version of yourself. Make sure that you are constantly growing and becoming better.

We must also spend time with our children. I know this can be difficult when they are little because of how busy we get with work and life, but it is imperative that we spend time with our children in order to teach them important lessons.

There's always been a debate about quality time versus quantity of time. I believe it needs to be both. I've always thought it would be funny to see a cartoon where a dad was sitting in his chair reading a book called *How to Be a Great Father* as his young child is standing there with a baseball glove asking him to go play. The dad tells him that he can't because he's reading a book about how to be a great father. You see, reading and thinking about it is not where it ends. You have to go and *do* it.

Understand that our roles transition as our children get older. We go from being director and protector to friend and advisor. It is a role that transitions from one to the other. Your role as protector and director doesn't just end one day, and then you're just their friend and advisor. It transitions. And, frankly, it's pretty fun. My children are grown now, and I like being able to be their friend and encourager and advisor.

It was interesting coming into my second marriage with Denise and being a stepfather to my two lovely stepdaughters. When I came into their lives, they were 17 and 15, and that had an interesting dynamic in the role I would play.

I told them once that being their stepdad was pretty easy because I didn't have to be their disciplinarian. Perhaps if we had gotten married when the girls were younger, say 6 and 4, I would most certainly have had to have filled a role as a disciplinarian, but since they were already incredible girls who had their heads on straight, I really didn't have to do any of that. It was freeing to me to know that I could just be their cheerleader, mentor, and friend.

You have to be purposeful. Yes, you have to plan to make a difference in your children's lives. You can't just fly by the seat of your pants and hope that they turn out all right. You need to give them direction. Of course, we should allow our children to make their own decisions as they get older, but we should still be there to give direction.

Sometimes I hear parents say that they will just let their children figure it out. For example, I see this with spirituality. I hear parents say they're just going to let their children figure it out. I would instead suggest that it's imperative that you teach your children about your religion because it is powerful for you—but, of course, to let them make their own decision in the end. They may or may not choose to follow the path of spirituality that you have, but at least you've been purposeful about passing it along while still giving them autonomy to become their own people.

Your children are waiting, hoping, and sometimes even begging for you to make a difference in their life. They want your impact. They want your love. If you want to make an impact, start with your own family. Make sure you do your best to help them become the people they were designed to be.

Questions for Reflection:

How do you impact your family?

Are you leaving a positive or negative impact?

What do you think of the statement that in order to teach right, you must first *be* right?

How do you spend both quality time and quantity of time?

What stage in your relationship with your children are you? How has it felt as you have transitioned?

Are you purposeful in your family relationships?

Chapter Nine

Grow Your Network

They say that your network is your net worth. And, to a great degree, that is true. It has also been said that you become like the five people you spend the most time with. Taking these two well-known sayings, you could come to the conclusion that your network is quite important for your life and wealth. But, your network is also imperative for your impact.

The people you come in contact and network with are a great resource for making an impact. First, *with* them, but second, they can open doors for you to make an even greater impact with others. I have found that to be true in my life to a great degree.

If you remember the old Six Degrees of Separation theory, it says that you should be within just six connections of anyone in the world. True networkers, people who know how to build out networks, can get themselves down to even second or third degrees of separation. I know that just in my personal life and business—let alone through the connections I have on Facebook and LinkedIn—I am only a couple of degrees away from almost anybody. That is a good thing for the life of my business!

It takes people to make an impact, so it makes sense that in order to make a giant impact, you should have a giant network. It makes sense that anytime you need something, you should be able to have people you can call on to help you make that happen.

This is one of the earliest things I learned in life, and perhaps it was from changing schools so often. I remained friends with people I knew going back to elementary school. I would move into a new school and become friends with people, but when I moved, I remained in touch with them. Then, with the advent of social media, it made it even easier to reconnect with people from my past. Sites like LinkedIn also make it very easy to connect with people you are interested in connecting with and may be able to do business with later on.

I have a friend, Joe Polish, who is the founder of the Genius Network. The Genius Network is one of the world's premier networking groups. Joe actually runs a number of different networking groups at various levels. These groups are so powerful that people pay him $100,000 a year to belong to one of his groups. Another of his groups costs $25,000 a year! I have another friend who belongs to the Genius Network, and he says that the five years he has written a check for $25,000 to Joe has been the best investment he's ever made in his business.

Imagine building out a network so valuable that people would be willing to pay $100,000 a year to be in it. But, if you think about it, it actually makes sense. For example, my friend who belongs to Joe's group is a professional business coach. To work with him costs $10,000 and up. He has found that being able to be around hundreds of success seekers allows him the ability to coach many of them in their speaking, and that's making belonging to Joe's group a profitable venture. Others may not do business in the group, but they do find the information and networking to be worth the money anyway, simply as an investment into their own personal and professional development.

So, what happens in a network, a networking group, or a Mastermind? It is the power of the collective. We are able to use our expertise to help others, but we also have the ability to be in relationship with other high achievers. These are the kinds of people who can give you great business and life advice.

You don't have to be in a high-end network in order to make an impact, but you do need to network. You do need to make sure that you are developing relationships with a wide variety of people who can improve your life and expand your impact.

To build your network, you have to network. Network can be both a noun and a verb. And in order for you to build the noun, you have to do the verb. You must network to build your network!

You have to get out there and reach out to people and make overtures to people you want to get into a relationship with. When I moved to Scottsdale, Arizona, I immediately began to build my network here. I had come from Seattle, where I was very well known. My network was as extensive as it could possibly get in Washington state. I was one degree of separation from almost anyone. In Scottsdale, however, hardly anyone knew me. So, what did I do? I got on LinkedIn and started reaching out to people in Scottsdale!

I simply did a LinkedIn search for people in Scottsdale. I searched for people who looked interesting or might have similar interests or goals and sent them a connection request. After that, I started taking people to lunch and coffee in order to get to know them better. It turned out to be an incredible idea. I've met and have begun to work with a great group of people here in Scottsdale. Some of us are even working on a project together! Some of the folks I met on LinkedIn and have developed friendships and working relationships with include the owner and president of one of the largest hotel developers here in the area, a former news anchor, a man who owns 42 restaurants, the number one CrossFit owner in America, professional athletes, and the mayor of Scottsdale. And that's just to name a few!

I even made a friendship with a man who's become a very dear friend. He is the rabbi of the fastest-growing Orthodox synagogue here in Scottsdale. He is one of the most cosmopolitan men I've ever met, having spent his life living all over the world and eventually doing his rabbinical studies in Milan, Italy. We met on LinkedIn and scheduled a meeting at a local Starbucks. I felt like I met my long-lost brother. Denise and I have since been invited many times to the rabbi's house for Shabbat dinner and were even invited to his daughter's Bat Mitzvah. It's been an incredible friendship that has developed. It has also opened up some business opportunities because, through getting to know me, the rabbi saw some things that I was working on and gladly made connections to some of the people he knows here in the Scottsdale area. One of the people he introduced me to works for one of these more well-known athletic clothing brands, and we are talking about doing a book together. That's the way the network works.

It's actually easy to build a network... if you know how. Here are a few tips to help you build your network.

Reach out to people. That's first and foremost. Some people will be interested, and some won't. No big deal on those who don't want to work with you. Work with those who are interested. People are open to people who approach them appropriately. If you're just approaching someone in order to sell them something, you can be sure that people will avoid you at all costs. But if you reach out to people and tell them that you'd like to get to know them and see if there might be a way you can serve them and their business, people are quite open to that. Just be natural and don't try to oversell.

Take them out for coffee or lunch. And you should pay! Get to know them. Schedule 30 or 45 minutes, but then let them go. You want to be appreciative and respectful of their time. Again, let me remind you that this is to get to know them and not to sell them something. In fact, sometimes, I will have a first appointment with someone, and when I tell someone else that I met with them, I will often be asked if I pitched them on something. My answer is always no. Why? Because they *expected* me to pitch them on something. And when I didn't, it made them feel as though I was interested in them and not just their money or business.

Ask them how you can help them. Don't ask them to help you. Ask for an opportunity to help them. When they give you something that you can do, do it. Oftentimes people will ask me how I was able to end up working with three of the top speakers and authors of the 20th century, John Maxwell, Zig Ziglar, and Jim Rohn. I believe the secret was in how I approached them.

You see, when people like that are approached by others in the same business who are not as successful as them, they typically hear something like this: "You are so successful. I would like to do what you do. Will you help me?" You need to realize that people like this are always being asked if they can help someone. They literally do not have the time to help everyone, so they usually turn them down.

I approach people like that in a different way. There is a subtle difference, but it makes all the difference. I ask successful people this question: "I would like to do what you do. How can I help you?"

Do you see the difference there? I'm not asking them to help me, which is what everybody else is asking, and they don't have the time to do. I'm asking how I can help *them*. And almost nobody is asking them that question.

John Maxwell needed someone to do some writing for him. The same is true with Jim Rohn. He needed someone to help him write the Jim Rohn One-Year Program and the book *Twelve Pillars*. He needed me to emcee his weekend leadership event. And I went on to do the last videotaped interview that Jim ever gave.

Zig Ziglar needed a co-host for his television show because he was getting older and didn't want to carry the show himself. I was willing to play second fiddle. In doing so, it opened up a world so big for me I couldn't have imagined it.

A few days later, send them a thank you and let them know that you appreciated their time. Too many people will have meetings with people and not even say thank you. Be sure to send a quick note. An email is fine. If they gave you their cell phone number, a text is fine, too. But what's really great is a handwritten note. That will set you apart from 99% of everyone else they have had coffee with lately.

Repeat as often as you need to, both with them and with new people. You will need to be relentless in building your network. You should always be taking people out for coffee or lunch or dinner. And of course, if it is for business, it is able to be written off on your taxes as business expenses!

Build relationships. Provide value. Be a servant. Those are the ways you build a network of interested and trusted people. As you build that relationship and provide beneficial help, eventually, that network is going to pay off and help you make your impact.

Once your network is built, you can take advantage of it. I don't mean that in a negative way, but you can take advantage of all of the resources available to you in a large and growing network. I'm at a place in my life where, having networked relentlessly for 30-plus years, I can get almost anyone for a meeting simply by utilizing the resources of my network.

My book *The Art of Influence* stems from someone noticing my extensive network.

When I was working with Jim Rohn International, the founder and president was a friend of mine named Kyle Wilson. We had been working together a couple of years, and I was thinking about writing my next book and creating my next audio program. Kyle suggested that I should do something on influence. I had been speaking on leadership and had written leadership books and done leadership seminars, but I'd never focused in on the influence aspect of leadership.

When I asked Kyle why he thought I should do that, he said it was because I was the only person he knew who could open his phone and call U.S. senators, billionaires, professional athletes, and CEOs of some of the biggest companies in the world. I had never really thought about it at that point, but I realized that I really was very good at building a powerful, large, and influential network.

So, I took six months and looked at my network-building habits and, specifically, the topic of influencing others. That became an audio program, a live seminar, and a book that has taken me all over the world.

I want you to make an impact, so I must implore you to spend time building your network. The size and strength of your network will be foundational to you in making your impact!

Questions for Reflection:

Do you agree that your network is your net worth?

How often do you reach out to people to create relationships?

Are you comfortable with asking people how you can help them?

Do you send thank you notes and follow up?

Chapter Ten

Plot Twist

They've said that the only thing that is sure about life is death and taxes, but I would also say that another sure thing is that no matter how life is going, there will be a series of plot twists that affect you in significant ways, both good and bad.

People who make a big impact are the people who successfully navigate the waters of the plot twists that take place in our lives. There are all sorts of plot twists that take place—cancer, bankruptcy, divorce, losing your job, and many others. People who can navigate those plot twists come back better and stronger.

Plot twists don't have to be negative. In fact, some are very positive. Positive plot twists will catapult you to greater success and impact, while negative plot twists need to be overcome, redirected, and refocused into furthering you along on your impact journey.

For example, I had a tremendously positive series of plot twists in the early 2000s. I was asked to write for John Maxwell, a best-selling leadership author. That was a tremendous opportunity and plot twist for me. After a couple of years, plot twist number two happened when I received a phone call from Kyle Wilson, the president of Jim Rohn International, asking me to write and co-author with Jim. And then, shortly after that, the third positive plot twist in just a number of years happened when I was asked to co-host Zig Ziglar's television show, True Performance. Prior to working with John, I had a relatively successful speaking business and was making ground. But with those three plot twists, my career catapulted.

Most of the time, though, the real battle is with the seemingly negative plot twist. And I say "seemingly" very purposefully because I believe that things may seem to be negative but, in fact, eventually lead to something very positive.

In my seminars, I will often reference the woman who started MADD (Mothers Against Drunk Drivers), Candy Lightner. Here is perhaps the absolute worst plot twist that could ever happen to a parent, burying their child, and even worse because she was killed in a senseless act. While the death of her daughter Cari would impact Lightner forever, she decided that she would make a difference. And, of course, we know what happened next. She created the greatest program encouraging people to not drink and drive the world has ever seen. That was a plot twist that seemed as though it could ruin the rest of her life, but she took it from something negative and made a significant positive impact on the world despite the negative circumstance.

Another example of navigating the plot twist is the life of my friend Andre Wadsworth. Andre played high school football and had some success, but wasn't recruited much and had to walk on to the Florida State football team. He barely made it as a freshman, but by the time he graduated, he was one of the best football players his university had ever produced.

In the 1998 NFL draft, Andre was taken 3rd overall, just behind Peyton Manning at number one and Ryan Leaf at number two. Andre signed a six-year, 42-million-dollar contract. Everything seemed incredible for Andre, and his future was as bright as it possibly could be.

Then, the injuries started. After three years of playing in the NFL and many surgeries on his knees, Andre was out of football.

Andre found himself asking the question that so many people do when they get hit with a negative plot twist: Now what do I do?

For many, it is to quit. They become so fearful and despondent and discouraged that they decide they won't pursue their big dreams anymore. They become victims rather than victors. People who make a great impact in their lives and businesses handle negative plot twists differently.

Fortunately, Andre had made great money from his being picked high in the draft and got into the car business.

But, it is what Andre is doing now—which was another plot twist in and of itself—that is really making an impact. Andre is a devout Christian man and was running a Bible study in the Phoenix area for professional athletes from the four major

Phoenix-area sports teams: the Cardinals, the Coyotes, the Suns, and the Diamondbacks.

Soon, with over a hundred people attending, they thought that perhaps they should start a church. And so, they did. They hired a preaching pastor, and Andre became the administrative pastor. That church is now one of the ten fastest-growing churches in America. Ironically, its name is Impact Church!

Every Sunday morning, just before you walk into the doors of the church, you will be greeted by a gentle giant, the six-foot-five, 280-pound former third pick in the NFL turned pastor, Andre Wadsworth. He'll give you a great big smile and hand you a bottle of water and welcome you to church. What seems like a negative plot twist for him has turned into something impacting thousands of people every week.

What does it take to navigate a plot twist? Well, it depends on whether it is positive or negative, so let's take a look.

Positive Plot Twists

Be thankful. The first thing we should always do is show gratitude. When life takes a turn for the better, we have to be purposeful about our thankfulness and gratitude. If something were to go negatively, many would naturally grumble and complain, so when something goes well, why isn't it that we are naturally thankful and filled with gratitude?

Don't fight it. When a positive plot twist happens, it's a little bit like riding a wave. Sometimes you don't know where it's going to take you because life has a funny way of taking us to places we didn't think we were going. So, when things are going well, yes, be looking ahead and making sure you're not headed toward danger but enjoy the ride and take the wave all the way to the shore.

Look forward as best you can. In many ways, the plot twist could take us to places we have no idea we are going to, but in other cases, if we look forward, we can see where we will eventually land. It's important to know where we're going to land to set us up for the next step.

Plot your strategy from your new landing place. Your new plot twist is going to take you to another level. Now that you've leveled up, how do you go further? What will be your strategy from your new position of strength? Understanding this will be the key to making sure you don't lose momentum in making your impact.

Negative Plot Twists

Stop the plot twist, if at all possible. For example, if your spouse gets sick, that's a plot twist, but it doesn't mean that you have to give into and accept the finality of it. You can fight it. And you should!

Limit the damage. If the situation cannot be turned back, then it is time to limit the damage. What can you do to keep this from being a negative or fatal plot twist?

Ask yourself what you can learn from the situation. Every negative situation still provides learning opportunities for those going through them. The worst situations in the world can turn into powerful opportunities when we are willing to look in the mirror and ask ourselves questions about what we are learning from the situation. How will this make us stronger? How will this make us smarter? How will this help us succeed in the future?

Look for the buried treasure. The stories of people who have turned negative circumstances into positive successes and impact are in the millions. The buried treasure for the woman who started MADD was that she helped hundreds of millions of people not to get behind the wheel drunk. The buried treasure for my friend Andre is that now he's helping thousands of people every week grow spiritually. There is always a buried treasure, and we can make good out of any negative plot twist.

Surround yourself with good counselors. When a negative plot twist takes place, we can turn inward, and being in a state of panic or fear can cause us to make poor decisions. We need to have smart people who are outside of the situation to give us the kind of advice we need to make it through.

Use the power of brokenness that comes from negative plot twists. One of the things you find from people who have gone through negative plot twists is that they are much more transparent, authentic, and human. This is one of the things that makes them so powerful. All of the peripheral falls away. Their focus can become lightning tight.

- The man who didn't spend enough time with his wife before she got sick changes, and he becomes a better man by being more devoted to her.

- The woman whose parents are trapped by Alzheimer's learns to become a servant and give back to her parents, who gave so much to her when she was a child.
- The man who is let go from his job of 20 years because of downsizing is finally forced to become an entrepreneur like he has always dreamed.

You were made to make an impact. You were designed to create a ripple that lasts long after you are gone. The journey is amazing. There are twists and turns and hills and valleys to go through. There will be plot twists all along the way. Successful people understand this before they start the journey. They prepare in advance, so they are able to make the changes they need to make when, all of a sudden, life or business is going in a different direction than they thought it would go.

Questions for Reflection:

What plot twists have you experienced in your own life or business? How did you handle them?

How have you handled negative plot twists?

What have you learned from the plot twists in your life that have enabled you to move forward and have greater impact?

What have been the buried treasures in your negative plot twists?

Have you surrounded yourself with good counselors to help you navigate negative plot twists?

Chapter Eleven

Sometimes Greatness Takes Time

Patience. It's a word we all know, but it's not a word that we deal with very well, is it? It seems as though we live in a day and age where we want everything, and we want everything *right now*! Unfortunately, significant impact usually takes time, and that means we have to learn patience.

Yes, occasionally, somebody will be living their daily life, and then some extraordinary event takes place, and they end up on the nightly news, making an impact worldwide. But this is, by far and away, the exception and not the rule.

True impact, the kind of impact that changes people's lives and leaves a ripple effect long after you are gone, is something that requires preparation, discipline, and follow-through. All of that takes time.

There is also another aspect that causes it to take time, and it is our own personal growth. Rarely do people impact the world at a younger age. The reason why is because we usually have to grow into our success, and one success builds on another until we have the most impact.

The key is to be able to live with the tension between contentment and ambition. Jim Rohn said that we should be "happy with what we have while we pursue all that we want."

Be patient. That's really good advice for anyone, and it is advice that we've been hearing since the time we were little kids. Our parents probably taught us that regularly. However, the being patient is also good for making an impact.

It seems as though we all want everything faster than that which we get it. I am as guilty as anybody. We want it *now*. But, it takes time to make an impact. Things build on each other and allow us to make a bigger impact later on.

In my book *The Angel Inside*, I go through life lessons from the life of Michelangelo. If you were to ask most people about Michelangelo and his art, they would likely mention one or two of his masterpieces. They will most likely mention the David in Florence, Italy, and the Sistine Chapel in the Vatican in Rome.

But, as I made clear in the book, no one begins with the Sistine Chapel. The Pope doesn't call up a newbie painter and ask him to come to the Vatican and do that kind of job. Michelangelo had to work himself up to the Sistine Chapel.

When Michelangelo was a young man, he created something that became popular called the Battle of the Centaurs. That is what gave him the credibility when he went to Rome to be commissioned with what I consider to be his most beautiful masterpiece, the Pieta. After creating the Pieta and returning to Florence, he was commissioned with the David, which has become one of the most recognizable statues in the world. It was only after doing the Battle of the Centaurs, the Pieta, the David, and hundreds of other small projects that Michelangelo had created the reputation that would garner him the invitation of the Pope at that time to paint the Sistine Chapel.

What is the lesson for us? Be patient. Do your best work now in order to create success later on. Your great work now will move you forward and open doors for you to do even greater work later. If you do poorly now and don't correct it or improve, you will never have the ability to do even greater things.

Many people become frustrated with the course they must take to make their big impact. By nature, we tend to want things to come as fast as they can, especially in this microwave world where we expect everything to happen quickly. Making a big impact is most often a long-term job and will require us to do smaller things on our journey. Many people become frustrated because they don't make a bigger impact early on.

It is the smaller things, though, that prepare us to make our big impact. Getting through the smaller things requires patience.

My friend Monty Wright began working in a grocery store in the town where we grew up in North Bend, Washington, at the age of 14. He started by simply bagging groceries and working the shelves at the grocery store. When he was old enough, he became a checker. At the same time, he had become a Christian and wanted to pursue ministry. All the while, he was preparing for ministry in Bible College, and as he began to work in churches as a worship pastor, he continued working at the grocery store to support his ministry.

Because he had not been able to go full-time in ministry due to the finances of the church he worked at, Monty continued to work as a checker in the grocery store. Even into his 30s, he was still working at the grocery store to make his money and working in ministry to make his impact.

This was frustrating for Monty. We had many conversations where he was frustrated that he had to continue working his job in the check stand at the grocery store. I kept telling him that eventually, this was going to pay off for him. Little did any of us know what would happen.

North Bend is a relatively small town with one main grocery store in it, although it has a few smaller grocery stores as well. Because Monty had been in this small town his entire life and his dad was well known for running one of the gas stations, everybody in town knew Monty, and most people in town came through his check stand at least once a week.

As Monty checked people out, he would ask about their lives. Little old ladies would talk about the issues they were going through, and young families would come through, and Monty would get to know the parents and the children. He would always listen and promise to pray for the problems people shared with him coming through his line.

Then, in 1999, Monty decided to start his own church in town. What happened next was pretty extraordinary and gave testament to the fact that working for twenty years in the grocery store was the very thing that would make him successful in his new church. Many of the people who went through Monty's line didn't go to church. They had no church association, but they liked Monty, and they were open to spirituality.

Monty very quickly built a congregation of hundreds of people because so many men and women who had never gone to church before decided they wanted to go simply because Monty was the pastor. Soon after, they bought their own building from a declining congregation, remodeled it, and it is now a packed house for both services on Sundays.

A couple of years into his new church, I went and visited his Sunday morning Easter Service. He held it in the local high school gymnasium, and there were seventeen hundred people there!

The lesson here is that while we don't see the grand plan, sometimes it's the little things that are preparing us for the wild success and impact we will have later on. All of those years of Monty ministering to people coming through his line, listening to them, giving them advice, and praying for them created a group of followers that would come around Monty and join his congregation when he finally opened the doors to the church. Monty's ministry continues to grow, and he has started a parachurch ministry called Planet Changers that helps people all over the world. The ministry is supported by the members of his congregation, many of whom had never gone to church before their grocery store checkout clerk became their pastor.

So, whether you are a Michelangelo in waiting or you are just trying to make your difference in the world around you, it is clear that there is usually a long build-up preparing you for your impact. Do not despise small beginnings or a long path on the way to your significant impact. It is all part of the journey.

Be patient as you travel the long road. Yes, set goals and monitor your progress, but understand that your impact will come from one small success built upon another small success until you reach your final goal.

Questions for Reflection:

How would you rate yourself on your level of patience?

How well do you do with the tension between contentment and ambition?

Where would you say you are in the trajectory of your life and business on the journey toward your Sistine Chapel?

Chapter Twelve

Focus on Legacy

It seems in recent times there has been an increasing emphasis on leaving a legacy. I don't know that there was a lot of discussion about it years ago, but it sure seems to be popular now. Everybody wants to know that they will be remembered in the minds of the people they leave behind when they pass on.

I am very aware of what legacy I will leave, mainly because my own father died when I was only four years old and left me without much in the memory department. Not only do I not remember much of anything I did with him—just a few memories are there—but he also didn't leave me anything to remember him by. That has always had a profound impact on the way I want to live my life so that my loved ones, and the world around me, are impacted by my having been here. This is why I have always thought, even from an early age, about the legacy I would leave behind.

It may seem like a strange way to remind myself, but I have developed an exercise that I practice from time to time to make me think through what kind of legacy I will leave. I occasionally imagine what the first Thanksgiving will be like for my family after I am gone. Now, be assured, I hope it isn't any time soon! I picture my whole family seated around the table, but with an empty chair where I would have been sitting. And then I wonder, "What will my family say about me? What will they miss? What will they long for?"

The answers to those three questions will give you amazing insights into the kind of life you are living right now and what kind of legacy you are probably going to leave.

Ask yourself, based on how you are living your life right now:

- How will people talk about you when you are gone?
- What will your family, friends, and co-workers miss about you?
- What will those closest to you long for when you are no longer able to be there?

If the answers you get satisfy you, then congratulations, you are set and good to go. If, however, what you come up with is less than stellar, then you have a few changes to make.

Here are a few thoughts on how to change so that you leave a fantastic legacy for others:

1. **Know that your legacy is based on what you do today.** If you want to leave a legacy of love, then love today. If you want to leave a legacy of financial success, then invest money today. If you want to leave a legacy of family time, then book that vacation today.

2. **Your legacy is the sum of the many days of your life added together.** Yes, there are a few folks who end up known forever through the history books (for good or for ill) because of one moment in time, but for most of us, it is the days of our lives, taken as a whole, that people remember. The point? Make it your goal to do something each and every day to build your legacy. If you want to be known as a kind person, do something kind each and every day for the people around you.

3. **Be a positive person and a source of happiness for those who come in contact with you.** The fact is, people want to be around positive people and they remember positive people more fondly than negative people. So, be positive!

Here's a blunt fact. You *will* leave a legacy. The question is really only whether or not it will be a good one. People will remember you. People will have an opinion of you. You get to determine now, as you build your legacy, how they will remember you. Keep that at the forefront of your mind on a daily basis so that you live in such a way every single day that it creates your legacy in the minds of other people.

I would like to close with a story that happened to me very early on in my career. It was weird at the time and still feels weird now, even though it profoundly affected me and how I perceive my life and career. You'll see why as you read the story.

I was at a conference in Edmonton, Alberta. I was just going along minding my own business when, during one of the breaks,

I turned around and there were two women right behind me, a mother and her daughter.

The daughter, who was about 30 years old, looked at me with stunned disbelief. Her eyes were wide open, and her jaw dropped. I felt a little strange. Her mother looked at her, then looked at me, then back at her and asked if I was the one.

"He's the one."

"So, tell him."

Strange, right?

The young woman proceeded to tell me that all throughout the night she couldn't sleep, restless, and when she finally fell asleep, she had a dream with a person she'd never met before and a message she was supposed to tell that person. She woke up and told her mother. Her mother suggested that she just keep her eyes open and that maybe there was something to it.

Less than 12 hours later, she was face-to-face with that person—me.

"I'm supposed to tell you that you should be a voice and not an echo."

At the time, I didn't know that this was a quote attributed to Albert Einstein. I was just a little weirded out. But, I must confess that, over the years, and this was 1989 by the way, I have repeatedly kept that advice near and dear to my heart and try to live by it. Especially in the speaking world, where there are so many people who are regurgitating motivational platitudes, I knew that to be successful, I would need to be that voice and not simply an echo of other people.

People who make an impact are trailblazers. They are not people who do what others do. They make their own way. They invent new things. They create. They take what is good, and they make it better. The travel the Lonely Road. They are not content to merely hear what others say and repeat it without thinking. Instead, they take what other people say, think it through, and come to a conclusion as to whether or not it is right or wrong. They come up with their own thoughts and ideas.

Is this you? Are you a voice? Or are you merely an echo? The world needs more people with creative voices. The world does not need more people who simply pass along what other people tell them.

This has been my calling and my goal throughout my career. I believe that the most impact is made when I am a voice and not merely an echo. I have always sought to say what others don't or won't. I haven't allowed myself to simply regurgitate what others have said but have tried to come up with my own take on things. I believe that will be my impact and my legacy.

I would like to challenge you to live this yourself. Be unique. Have a unique voice. Make it heard. Leave a legacy and make an impact!

Questions for Reflection:

How do you feel you are doing living your life and running your business so that you will leave the legacy you want to leave?

What areas of your life do you need to work on to make sure you leave the legacy you want to leave?

Are you a voice, or an echo?

Chapter Thirteen

Ready, Set, Go!

Congratulations, you got through the book! Now the real work begins—you have to take it from intellectual assent and agreement to actions that are going to create the future that you desire.

Here are some suggestions for you as you move forward:

First, **get clear with your purpose and your mission**. You need to begin with the end in mind and know what it is that you want to do. If you need to incorporate a spouse or business partner, that's great. Do it. And do it soon.

Second, **create a plan and a strategy**. You need to know exactly how you're going to get there. It's sort of like a road trip you might take. You may say that you're going to drive to Chicago. That's your ultimate destination, but how are you going to get there? What roads are you going to take? Where will your stops be? We plan out our road trips, so why don't we plan out our impact?

Collect your resources. This is your money, your skill-set, your partners, and all of the things you are going to use as resources to make your impact.

Go to work. Most impact takes a long time. Great impact takes an even longer time. You're going to have to work and work hard and do it for a long time.

Establish a way to analyze your progress. From time to time, you're going to have to look and see how you're doing. And from there you're going to have to make changes if you find yourself off course.

Persevere. You're going to face obstacles. You're going to fail from time to time. People will disappoint you. All of that is okay because your impact is important enough to make sure you don't quit.

Enjoy the journey. Life is short, and it is designed to be joyous and fulfilling. Don't take yourself too seriously. Do great things and live a great life. Live, laugh, and love to the greatest degree that you can.

I want to thank you for reading this book. I am passionate about helping people make a lasting impact. I'm dedicated to making a lasting impact myself. May your impact be great, and may you change the lives of the people around you. May you make the world a better place than it was when you entered into it.

An Additional Word

"The greatest legacy one can pass on to one's children and grandchildren is not money or other material things accumulated in one's life, but rather a legacy of character and faith."

— Billy Graham

At this point, I'm going to give you a choice. You can choose to close the book and go on your way with what you have read so far. Or, you can continue reading. I feel it's important to let you know about what I'm going to write about next because I do know that the topic can cause some people uneasiness.

I want to talk to you about faith. Specifically, my Christian faith. Again, no problem if you aren't interested and you close the book right now. I would be remiss, however, if I didn't include an additional word about my faith because it is so important in regard to how I think about impact.

So, for those of you who want to close the book, that's totally fine. For those of you who are interested in the story of my faith and how it drives my desire for impact, read on...

As you've read, I had a crazy upbringing. I knew nothing about God. One Saturday night, in my sophomore or junior year of high school, I was spending the night with one of my good friends who I regularly drank and used drugs with. On Sunday morning, his mother threw open the door, woke us up, and announced that we were all going to something she called "Sunday school." I truly had no clue what Sunday school was. It was bad enough that I had to go to Monday through Friday school! Those of you who grew up in the church probably chuckled a little bit there. But it's true. I had no experience with church, and I had no idea what Sunday school was.

When I started attending there, we would sometimes go to youth group drunk. It wasn't a pleasant situation. Especially for the youth minister who seemed to not be able to control the youth group. Eventually, we got a new youth minister. His name was Sam, and he was a good old boy from Montana. Sam was exactly what I needed. First of all, he was a great male role model. I didn't have a lot of older males in my life. One grandfather divorced my grandmother and moved away, and I had only met him one time in my entire life. My other grandfather died when I was a young boy, and I hardly ever interacted with him before he died because he had emphysema so bad he just laid on the couch with his oxygen mask on. I didn't see my uncles much, and my brother, who is 13 years older than me, married a girl who didn't like my mother at all, so we didn't see them very often. Now, I had a youth minister who was a great male role model, and in some ways, a father figure.

Sam also taught me about God and His son Jesus. I had never really thought about it. I had never heard about it. He began to teach me the Bible, and I begin to study it for myself. It made sense to me. It seems unbelievable to me that anyone could look at the complexity of our world and believe that it all just randomly happened. I believe that the evidence proves there is at least an intelligent designer, as many of the world's greatest scientists believe. They look at science, the world, and the universe and they realize that the probability of this randomly happening is virtually none.

I believe in a personal God. I don't believe in what people call the "Universe." I believe the universe is a place, not a person. I believe that calling it "the universe" does a disservice to you because it keeps a personal God who, according to the Bible, even knows the number of hairs on your head, at a distance. It makes God "out there" somewhere. God knows your thoughts before you even have them. The Bible tells us that God wants to have a relationship with us, and that's why He sent His son Jesus. Calling God the universe is impersonal, and the God of the universe is a personal God!

After coming to an understanding of the God who loves me and Jesus who died for me, I gave my life to the Lord in the summer of 1983.

Now, some people tell you that when they committed their lives to the Lord, everything was great from then on out. That would not be my story. I am far from a perfect Christian. But I take joy in knowing that in my weakness, God shows his strength.

I have had a lot of highs as a Christian, and especially as a minister. I've been able to officiate at weddings and baptize people. I've celebrated with people during the greatest times of their lives.

I've also had a lot of lows. I've had to help my parishioners, and even in affluent churches filled with successful people, there are lots of problems. I've found myself in the door of drug dens in downtown Seattle searching for men who attended my church in order to get them back to their families. As a police chaplain for the Issaquah Police Department, I was there when families called us after they found one of their loved ones that committed suicide.

The same is true in my personal walk with Christ. I have had lots of joy. I've seen God work in my life and give me faith and courage to do great things. God gave me the gift of being able to speak. I do not take pride in some of the accolades I have received as a speaker because I know that they are a gift from someone else. I truly do humbly use that gift to help others.

And I've had some bad times as a Christian as well. I have failed God miserably numerous times. I have gotten angry at God because life wasn't going the way I wanted it to. After 27 years, my first marriage failed. Imagine the pain, shame, embarrassment, and suffering that comes when you are a well-known pastor who goes through a divorce. It was horrible.

Thankfully, God is the God of second chances. Frankly, he's also the God of third, fourth, fifth, and more chances, too!

Going through hardships has caused me to hold on to God for dear life. Going through hardships taught me to be compassionate and kind. I'm much more forgiving and accepting. I know that if God can forgive me for so much, I must be willing to forgive others.

I don't know you, who you are, or really anything about you, but I do know that you were created for impact. You were created by a loving God who knows you and has a specific plan for you. He has given you gifts and talents specifically so you can make an incredible impact in your time here. It is His plan for you!

One of the reasons I can have such a big impact is because I go into my daily life knowing that God *wants* me to make an impact. I know that He has forgiven me, continues to forgive me, and blesses me with gifts and talents that will help others. I need to stay right with Him, close to Him. That is my major goal going forward in my life. Stay close to the Lord and follow His leading.

I would challenge you to consider Jesus again. Some of you are reading this and you already have a relationship with the Lord, and that is fantastic. I want you to be blessed and make the impact that God has planned for you. Some of you reading this have made a commitment to the Lord, but you are elsewhere as you read this. I know you want to have an impact. That desire was given to you by God. But you need to turn back to Him and get right with Him so you can fulfill *His* plan for your life.

Then, there are those of you who are reading this who have never had a relationship with Jesus. You don't know anything about the Bible. That's okay. Now you know. I'm telling you that there is a God and that He is a personal God and that He wants to have a relationship with you. He's waiting with open arms to receive you when you come to Him. I would like to challenge you to study the Bible and learn about the person of Jesus. I made the best decision of my life that warm summer evening in 1983. Everything changed from that point forward. During the great times, I was grateful. During the down times, I know that God was walking with me, taking care of me, and leading the way so that I could fulfill his plan and purpose in my life and make an impact in the lives of others. And now, He wants to do the same with you!

About Chris

 **Chris Widener** is widely recognized as one of the top personal development influencers in the world. He's been named one of the top 50 speakers in the world, one of Inc. Magazine's Top 100 Leadership Speakers, and is a member of the Motivational Speakers Hall of Fame. Chris has written 21 books that have been translated into 14 languages. Chris also has a small boutique coaching practice where he works one on one with successful entrepreneurs and executives to help them improve their lives and business. Chris and his wife Denise reside in beautiful Scottsdale, Arizona.

Are you looking to take your life and business to the next level and beyond?

Are you ready to create a life and business that lives beyond you? Now, you have the opportunity to work personally, one-on-one, with famed motivator Chris Widener. Chris will teach you and help you implement all of the important lessons you've learned in *Lasting Impact.*

To set up your personal discovery call to inquire about working with Chris, you may call 1-877-212-4747 or send an email to Chris@ChrisWidener.com.

Other
Chris Widener Books/Audiobooks

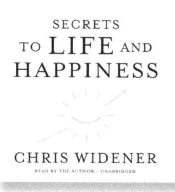

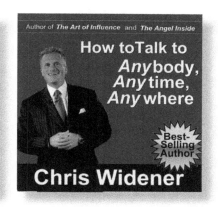

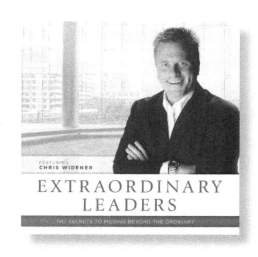

CPSIA information can be obtained
at www.ICGtesting.com
Printed in the USA
FSHW021111111220

9 781641 464765